ARCHAEOLOGY

ΑΙΝΩΝ ΕΝΘΑ
ΝΥΝ Ο CΑΠCΑ
ΦΑ

ΒΕΘΑΒΑΡΑ
ΤΟΤΥΑΓΙΥ ΙΩΑΝΝΟΥ
ΤΥΒΑC ΠΤΙCΜΑ
ΤΟC
ΑΛΩΝΑΤΑΘΗΝΥΜ
ΒΗΘΑΛΛ

ΤΟΚΑΙ
ΓΕΟΝ

ΙΕΡΙΧΩ

ΡΕΜΜΟΝ Η ΛΙΜΝΗ ΤΟΝΑΓ Η
ΜΟΖΑ ΚΑΙ ΒΕΘΛ

Η ΠΗΓΗ ΤΟΦΝ

ΡΕΜΜΟΝ
ΜΟΖΑ ΚΑΙ ΒΕΘΛ

ΠΡΟΒΗΧ

Η ΑΓΙΑ ΠΟΛΙΣ ΙΕΡΟΥCΑ

ΟΤΟ Η ΠΗΓΗ ΤΟΦΝΑ
ΟΤΟ Η ΠΗΓΗ ΤΟΦΝΥ

Ι Θ ΙΙΒ

ARCHAEOLOGY

Discovering the World's Secrets

GAYNOR AALTONEN

ARCTURUS

This book is dedicated to Isobel

Author's Acknowledgments
With thanks to all who contributed, but a special word
of thanks in no particular order to William Aaltonen,
Vanessa Daubney, John Turing and Charles T. G. Clarke.

Publishers' Acknowledgments
The publishers would like to thank the following people
for their help in supplying material for this book: The
Archaeological Survey of India; Professor Jack Davis, Dr
Shari Stocker and Carol Hershenson of The Department
of Classics, University of Cincinnati; Ingemar Lundgren;
M. Jean Michel at ArchéoJuraSites; Dr Matthew Nicholls
at The University of Reading; Oxford Archaeology;
Biagio Sol and everyone at BaiaSommersa, and Karolina
Mikulska at Världskulturmuseerna.

ARCTURUS

This edition published in 2017 by Arcturus Publishing Limited
26/27 Bickels Yard, 151–153 Bermondsey Street,
London SE1 3HA

ISBN: 978-1-78428-772-6
AD005615UK

Printed in China

CONTENTS

Introduction

"Order is Heaven's first law"
Alexander Pope

Archaeology opens windows into the past. It allows us to wonder at the riches of Tutankhamun's tomb, feel the pathos of the medieval serf scratching a living from feudal soil and marvel at the sublime cave art of the hunter-gatherer. From its beginnings, archaeology has challenged established views by ordering, analysing and rigorously re-ordering the evidence of the past, transforming our view of the ancient world. Piece by painstaking piece, it has helped us to reconstruct and understand human life, and rewrite the history of *Homo sapiens*.

Archaeology in the 21st century is a rigorous and demanding discipline. Trying to decipher the human past requires a broad range of skills, framed by scientific methods. The sense of mystery and the drama of an important find are still there, but they go hand in hand with methodical scholarship and sheer hard work. Huge advances in science are helping us to find, understand and reinterpret the past, which has plenty to say about subjects that have resonance for today's world, such as climate change. Archaeology gives us access, in other words, to a vast store of human experience.

New Discoveries and Challenges

Some archaeological stories have only just begun and their tales will unfold and change over the next few decades – from the submerged city of Baiae, one of the most notorious flesh-pots of Ancient Rome, to Israel's Tel Zafit National Park, in which lies the ancient city of Gath, the home town of the biblical Philistine giant, Goliath, to the Mesoamerican city of Tlaxcallan, which Mexico's Centre for Research and Advanced Studies of the National Polytechnic Institute believe was one of several pre-modern societies that were collectively organized and ruled.

In Uzès, in the south of France, an entire new Roman town – Ucetia – has been discovered hidden beneath the car park and surrounding grounds of a provincial school containing artefacts ranging from the 1st century BCE, the era of the Roman Republic, right through to the Middle Ages. While the difficulties in preserving Fort Conger in the Arctic, where Robert Peary was once based and which is now in danger from rising sea levels and salt deterioration, have led the University of Calgary to document the entire site in virtual reality, using three-dimensional imaging techniques.

Excavations can take years; evidence can be misleading. The key to successful archaeology is patience, persistence and an open mind. This book will take you on a journey back in time to visit ancient cultures and view different landscapes. It will also introduce an amazing array of characters, people who have braved desert storms, penetrated terrifying underground tombs and spent entire personal fortunes to bring us face to face with our ancestors. It even takes a detour into bad archaeology, via World War II and the Nazi Party. Archaeology is a vast subject: any period or region could easily fill an entire book, so here we explore this fascinating world through some of archaeology's most exciting highlights.

OPPOSITE
A detail from one of the mosaic floors discovered in the ruins of the Roman town of Ucetia that was revealed in Uzès in southern France

WHAT IS ARCHAEOLOGY?

"Wonderful things," breathed Howard Carter when he first made out the glittering treasures inside Tutankhamun's tomb. The treasure archaeologists find may amaze and delight us, but more important still is the light that scientific study sheds on the past.

The word "archaeology" comes from the Greek words *arkhaios* (meaning "ancient") and *logos* (meaning the "word", "reason", or "plan"). The Greeks used the term as early as the 4th century BCE to mean the study of the very ancient past.

Archaeologists often work in multi-disciplinary teams, because it's one of the few areas of enquiry that touches the humanities, natural sciences and social sciences. The study also frequently depends on international partnerships, since today's civilizations don't always respect the boundaries of earlier ones. Archaeologists may also specialize in a certain time period, a geographic area, a cultural tradition or some other sub-discipline such as maritime archaeology.

What archaeologists don't do, despite what everyone sees in the media, is study dinosaurs. In the field, it may be difficult to tell the difference between a palaeontologist and an archaeologist – sunhats and shorts look pretty much the same the world over – but archaeologists do not puzzle over Titanosaurs or Pteradactyls. They would be 65 million years out of their depth. The discovery of dinosaur remains does have a bearing on our understanding of geological, "deep" time, however, and therefore on the history of archaeology.

The material that archaeologists uncover helps them to piece together a living picture of the past. Tools and pottery sherds can tell us huge amounts about the domestic and economic customs of a given civilization; sculptures and artwork enlighten us about religious, spiritual and cultural practices; while weapons and armour offer new insights into ancient warfare.

The difference between history and archaeology comes down to written records. History records the past as set down in writing, oral accounts or documents, while the term "prehistory" covers the period before people began to document their lives. Archaeology spans both. Mediaeval Europe, with its scribes and scholars, is open to historical study, while the Americas of the same period are the sole concern of archaeology.

Nowadays, archaeologists have a raft of new technologies to aid them in their searches, from aerial photography to ground-penetrating radar, lasers and even robots. These new and ever more sophisticated techniques mean that not only are archaeologists now producing increasingly accurate data, but they are also helping us to rewrite history altogether.

BELOW
Getting down to business: an archaeologist uncovers a piece of pottery during an excavation.

OPPOSITE
A gold Inca mask. In Inca culture, masks were used either as part of rituals to worship gods such as Inti, the sun god, or as funerary masks.

TYPES OF ARCHAEOLOGY

Today, archaeology has obtained a bewildering array of prefixes. There is bioarcheology, behavioural archaeology, ethnoarchaeology, maritime archaeology and geoarchaeology amongst others. The methods used are as complex and varied as the archaeologists who use them. Nonetheless, whatever their methods, at the heart they aim to illuminate our understanding of the past through studying its material remains. Most prefixes simply refer to the methods used to uncover the past, but here are a few of the most important:

HISTORICAL ARCHAEOLOGY
The study of the material past of civilizations that also created written records.

MARITIME ARCHAEOLOGY
The study of submarine archaeological sites such as shipwrecks and sunken cities.

ETHNOARCHAEOLOGY
The study of modern societies that resemble extinct ones.

AERIAL ARCHAEOLOGY
The study of archaeological sites from aerial photography.

ENVIROMENTAL ARCHAEOLOGY
The study of relationships between humans and their environment.

PALEOPATHOLOGY
The study of ancient diseases.

ARCHAEOLOGY TIMELINE

This timeline aims to give an overview of the periods that this book touches on. It also highlights many, but by no means all, of the most important discoveries and developments in archaeology across the globe. The results of new research and new archaeological finds mean that this is an ever-changing story.

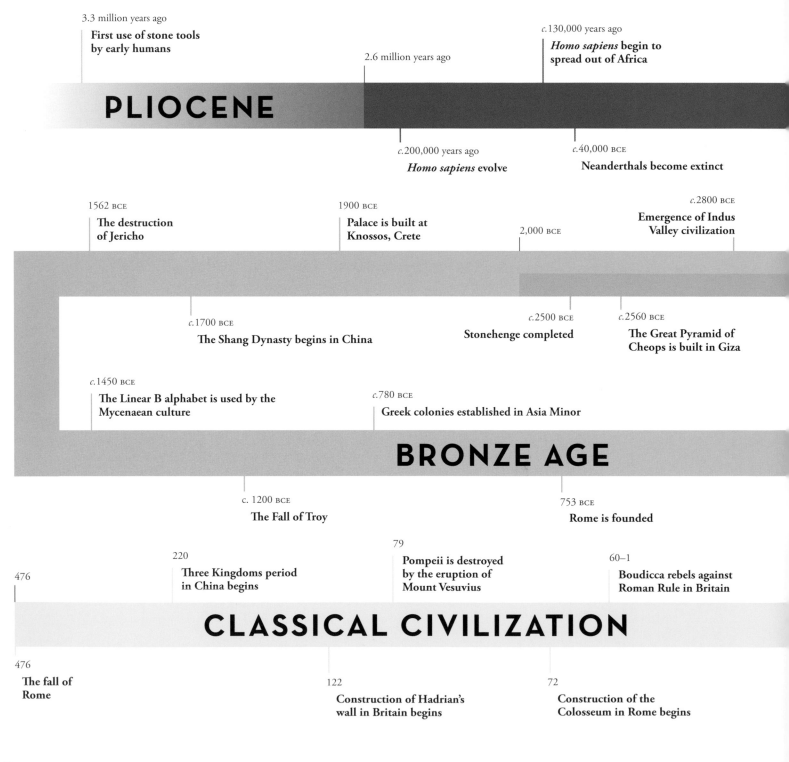

3.3 million years ago
First use of stone tools by early humans

2.6 million years ago

c.130,000 years ago
Homo sapiens begin to spread out of Africa

c.200,000 years ago
Homo sapiens evolve

c.40,000 BCE
Neanderthals become extinct

PLIOCENE

1562 BCE
The destruction of Jericho

1900 BCE
Palace is built at Knossos, Crete

2,000 BCE

c.2800 BCE
Emergence of Indus Valley civilization

c.1700 BCE
The Shang Dynasty begins in China

c.2500 BCE
Stonehenge completed

c.2560 BCE
The Great Pyramid of Cheops is built in Giza

c.1450 BCE
The Linear B alphabet is used by the Mycenaean culture

c.780 BCE
Greek colonies established in Asia Minor

BRONZE AGE

c. 1200 BCE
The Fall of Troy

753 BCE
Rome is founded

220
Three Kingdoms period in China begins

79
Pompeii is destroyed by the eruption of Mount Vesuvius

60–1
Boudicca rebels against Roman Rule in Britain

476

CLASSICAL CIVILIZATION

476
The fall of Rome

122
Construction of Hadrian's wall in Britain begins

72
Construction of the Colosseum in Rome begins

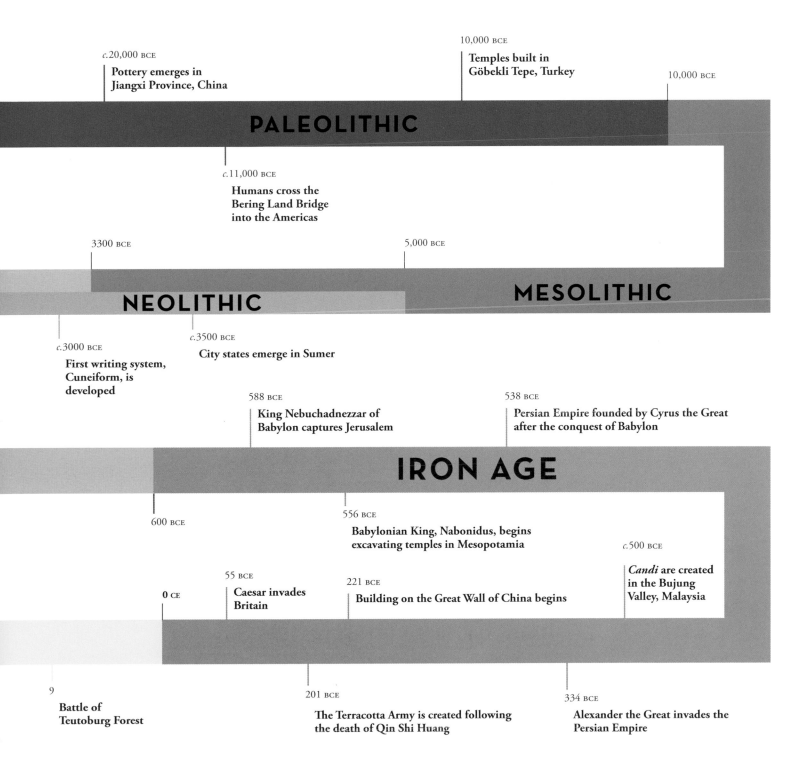

c.20,000 BCE
Pottery emerges in Jiangxi Province, China

10,000 BCE
Temples built in Göbekli Tepe, Turkey

10,000 BCE

PALEOLITHIC

c.11,000 BCE
Humans cross the Bering Land Bridge into the Americas

3300 BCE

5,000 BCE

NEOLITHIC

MESOLITHIC

c.3000 BCE
First writing system, Cuneiform, is developed

c.3500 BCE
City states emerge in Sumer

588 BCE
King Nebuchadnezzar of Babylon captures Jerusalem

538 BCE
Persian Empire founded by Cyrus the Great after the conquest of Babylon

IRON AGE

600 BCE

556 BCE
Babylonian King, Nabonidus, begins excavating temples in Mesopotamia

c.500 BCE
***Candi* are created in the Bujung Valley, Malaysia**

0 CE

55 BCE
Caesar invades Britain

221 BCE
Building on the Great Wall of China begins

9
Battle of Teutoburg Forest

201 BCE
The Terracotta Army is created following the death of Qin Shi Huang

334 BCE
Alexander the Great invades the Persian Empire

793
Viking raid on
Lindisfarne island

868
The first printed work, the
Diamond Sutra, is printed in
India

1088
Shen Kuo sets
out a theory of
archaeology in the
Dream Pool Essays

476

1000

THE MIGRATION PERIOD (THE DARK AGES)

476
The fall of
Rome

865
Great Heathen
Army arrives on
English shores

899
Tikal is abandoned along
with other Mayan cities

c.1000
Leif Erikson reaches L'Anse aux
Meadows in Newfoundland

1092
Lü Dalin creates the
first archaeological
catalogue

1876
The Battle of Little
Bighorn

1865
The Palestine Exploration
Fund is created

1856
Alexander Cunningham
founds the Archaeological
Survey of India

1834
Stephens and Catherwood
uncover the ruins of
Mayan cities in the
Yucatan jungle

1822
Champollion
deciphers the
Rosetta Stone

INDUSTRIAL ERA

1871
Heinrich Schliemann
excavates Troy

1861
Johann Fuhlrott
discovers the first
Neanderthal skeleton

1836
Christian Thomsen
explains "The Three Age
System" for the first time

1826
Charles Masson
discovers evidence of the
Indus Valley civilization

1819
John Smith
discovers the
Ajanta caves

1880
Sir William Flinders Petrie
surveys the pyramids at Giza

1892
Max Uhle
excavates the site
of Tiwanaku

1900
Sir Arthur Evans
excavates and
restores Knossos

1914

1877
Edward Morse
excavates the Omori
Shell Mounds

1883
Frederic Ward Putnam
begins excavating
Serpent Mound in Ohio

1899
Oracle bones are
discovered at Yinxu

1900
Divers find the Antikythera
mechanism in a shipwreck

1911
Hiram Bingham
uncovers Machu Picchu

1996
Kennewick Man is
found in the Columbia
River in the USA

2009
Staffordshire Hoard found
from 7th and 8th centuries

1998
The "Artognou" stone
is unearthed at Tintagel

Present

2016
In Sohag, Egypt, a
7,000-year-old city is
discovered

2012
The skeleton of King
Richard III is found
in Leicester

2008
Marge Konsa excavates Viking
ships found at Salme, Estonia

1994
The Jamestown Rediscovery
Project is launched

c.1150

Angkor Wat is
constructed

1438

The Inca Empire
begins after Cuzco's
conquest of the
Chanka

1450

1485

Battle of
Bosworth Field

1532

Francisco Pizarro
conquers the Inca

MEDIEVAL ERA

RENAISSANCE

1368

Ming Dynasty
overthrows Mongols

1440

The rise of the
Aztec Empire

c.1450

The building of Machu
Picchu begins

1521

Tenochtitlan falls to
Spanish Conquistadors

1799

French soldiers find
Ancient Egyptian artefacts

1815

1721

William Stukeley
excavates
Stonehenge

1691

The British Levant Company
sends an expedition to Palmyra

1700

ENLIGHTENMENT

1812

Johann Ludwig Burckhardt
discovers Petra

1748

Pompeii is excavated
by Karl Weber

1707

Edmund Halley attempts to discover
the origins of Stonehenge

1607

Jamestown, the first
English settlement in the
Americas, is founded

1921

Johan Gunnar Andersson
and Yuan Fuli investigate
the Yellow River culture
in China

1924–1926

K. N. Dikshit and John
Marshall excavate
Mohenjo-Daro

1933

Polish archaeologists led
by Józef Kostrzowski
excavate Biskupin

1939

Basil Brown excavates the
Saxon hoard at Sutton Hoo

MODERN ERA

1922

Howard Carter discovers
Tutankhamun's tomb

1929

Louis Leakey discovers stone
tools in the Olduvai Gorge

1938

Heinrich Himmler
launches a Nazi
archaeological expedition
to the Himalayas

1939

Theodore Morde claims
to have discovered
"The Lost City of the
Monkey God"

1987

Walter Alva saves the Lord
of Sipán archaeological site
from looters

1978

The Templo Mayor
is found beneath the
roads of Mexico City

1956

Excavation of the
Dingling Tomb begins

1940

Marcel Ravidat
discovers Lascaux Cave
paintings in France

1987

The Nanhai No. 1 ship
is found in the South
China Sea

1974

Archaeologists in
Xi'an, China excavate
the Terracotta Army

1962

Excavation of the
Manunggul caves in
the Philippines begins

1946

The Dead Sea Scrolls
are discovered

A FASCINATION
WITH THE PAST

A Fascination with the Past

The very first people to discover the great tombs of Egypt were driven not by curiosity but by greed. They were literally gold diggers, opportunistic thieves. Although the Pharoahs and the zealous priests who guarded the tombs did everything they could to warn the robbers off, they met with little success. An inscription in the tomb of Vizier Khentika Ikhekhi at Saqqara – behind two sets of false doors – reads: "As for all men who shall enter this my tomb… there will be judgment… an end shall be made for him."

A papyrus documenting a trial, and the "double-rod" beating before it, from the time of Ramesses IX (1142–23 BCE) tells us that thieves broke into hundreds of tombs, including those of Amenophis III, Seti I and Ramesses II. The confessions of the stonecutter Hap, the water carrier Kemwese, the artisan Iramen, the peasant Amenemheb and the Negro slave Thenefer give a graphic account of the problem the Pharaohs faced: "We opened their coffins and their coverings. We found the august mummy of this King… there was a numerous string of amulets and ornaments of gold at its throat; its head had a mask of gold upon it… We stripped off the gold, we found the king's wife likewise and stripped off all that we found. We… stole their furniture, being vases of gold, silver and bronze."

Even today, villagers from modern-day Gurnah, which is built over and around the remarkable ruins at Karnak in Upper Egypt, have been imprisoned for scavenging the treasure that Egypt now regards as its national heritage.

There has always been tension between the desire to collect the treasures of ancient cultures and the yearning to understand what they say about human life. The two instincts might seem contradictory, but perhaps one reason why archaeology is so popular is that it serves both of these perfectly human impulses well.

Many of the prized historic objects we now put on pedestals in museums were once pure loot. The Roman Emperor Constantine helped himself to the very tallest obelisk from the magnificent

temple complex at Karnak and installed it in the middle of Rome (where it is now known as the Lateran Obelisk). Alexander the Great plundered the jewel of Persia, Persepolis, known as the "wealthiest city under the sun". Even the sublime alert bronze horses that crown Venice's Basilica of Saint Mark were stolen from Constantinople during the Crusades. Somehow, they never made it back. Looted in turn by Napoléon, they were removed to Paris, and then returned – to Venice – on his downfall.

In 16th-century England, Dr Dee, Elizabeth I's handsome alchemist-cum-astrologer and advisor, straddled both camps. Dee claimed to predict the future, talking to angels through the swirling reflections he called up from a sinister "magic" mirror. We now know this was a piece of polished obsidian, once used in

OPPOSITE RIGHT
Roman contol of Egypt from 30 BCE triggered an infatuation with all things Egyptian. This obelisk originally stood at the east end of the Temple of Amun in Karnak, where it symbolized the Pharoah's connection with the gods; it was moved to the Circus Maximus in ancient Rome, and today, topped with a cross, stands in the Piazza San Giovanni. Rome still has more obelisks than any other city.

ABOVE
The proud bronze horses that adorn Venice's Basilica of Saint Mark may originally have been sculpted by Greek hands – a dramatic piece of Crusader booty.

RIGHT
In acquisitive Tudor England, Elizabeth I's alchemist acquired a sacred mirror, possibly Aztec, which became known as his "black stone". Dr Dee conjured spells via volcanic obsidian, which today features as "dragon glass" in the novel/TV series *Game of Thrones*.

the ancient rituals of an Aztec god. How Dr Dee came by such a precious thing we do not know; the Spanish conquistadors probably stole it in South America.

During the Renaissance, rich Italian families began amassing large collections of ancient Classical art, much of which was lying buried beneath their feet. Lorenzo de' Medici's famous library and gardens in Florence were full of ancient Greek and Roman sculpture. In Aix-en-Provence, the great intellectual Nicolas-Claude Fabri de Peiresc turned his entire home into a gallery and museum of Classical works. As European royal families struggled to establish national and military supremacy, ancient art became a quick way of both making money and also acquiring a veneer of legitimacy. In the 15th century, King Matthias I of Hungary kept his huge collection of Roman antiquities at Szombathely, a castle built with stone from the town's Roman baths. It is still there, and now a museum.

Eventually, there came a dawning interest in actually studying history and culture to understand them, and a realization that the great monuments of civilization should not be lost. In the early 16th century Pope Leo X commissioned the painter Raphael to study and document all the monuments of Rome, putting an end to the uncontrolled plunder of the city's rich heritage.

The "Cabinet of Curiosities"

In 1605, a young Danish physician and natural philosopher, Ole Worm, inherited a fortune and set out across Europe to continue his education. Worm became one of the world's first serious scientific collectors, creating what could be called the first museum.

A philosopher, physician and dedicated linguist, Worm's defining characteristic was his amazing, boundless curiosity – and his painstakingly accurate methodology. By studying with a new scientific rigour subjects such as "unicorns' horns" or the evolutionary adaptation of birds-of-paradise, Worm pre-empted the rational values of the coming Age of Enlightenment by a hundred years.

Nationalism also played its part. A wide-ranging report that Worm wrote on the ancient monuments of Denmark aroused the interest of King Frederik III. Frederik realized that this cultural heritage could be useful in uniting the uneasy "Two Kingdoms" of Norway and Denmark. The use of science, culture and archaeology as potent propaganda tools in Scandinavia set a precedent in Europe, although this did

OPPOSITE
This sculpture of the Trojan priest Laocoön and his sons being attacked by snakes was unearthed in a Roman vineyard during the Renaissance. Michelangelo was called to the scene, and the sculpture was put on display in the Vatican, where it remains.

RIGHT
A "cabinet of curiosities" from a private collection. It includes some coral, a Buddhist idol and skulls of a macaw, an ostrich and a human medical specimen. If this were not eclectic enough, there are also a Chinese clock, giant barnacles and a mammoth tooth.

not prevent Frederik from commissioning a throne chair made entirely from the horns of the mythical "unicorn" 30 years after Worm had correctly identified them as narwhal horns.

Ranging from fossils to stuffed animals, along with bizarre ethnographic treasures found in the New World, this hugely influential Renaissance man's collection, and the documentation that went with it, helped bridge the divide between science and mere curiosity. Which does not mean there were not some very curious exhibits: Worm owned what may well have been the world's first robot, a *statua librata pondre mobilis* – a wheeled figure with flexible limbs that could pick things up – as well as an "egg" supposedly laid by a Norwegian, Anna Omundsdatter. The egg came with sworn witness testimonials as to its miraculous appearance, including one by a parish priest.

As a naturalist and antiquarian, Worm was in the vanguard of a developing wave of scientific enquiry across Europe. The significance of this for archaeology lay in the way that he categorized and ordered his vast collection. Apart from coins and objects that were unclassifiable, he listed the eclectic mix of things by their different materials: clay, wood, bronze, stone, iron and so on. This set a precedent for more rigorous enquiry.

In response to the methodology by which Worm ordered his collections, another Dane, Christian Jürgensen Thomsen,

developed the Three Ages dating system (still used today) as a way of classifying archaeological finds. As Director of the Royal Museum of Nordic Antiquities in Copenhagen, Thomsen was keen to display objects from prehistory in a rational order that would help people understand them. He came up with the relative system of a Stone Age, Bronze Age and Iron Age, based on the main technologies that people were using at different times. Even if dating systems are now far more complex, this was a real innovation.

Worm's extraordinary collection was later part of the Royal Danish *Kunstkammer* (Art Chamber). His "cabinet" has been painstakingly re-created by the artist Rosamond Purcell at the Natural History Museum of Denmark in Copenhagen, where polar bears and crocodiles hang from rafters, and skulls (both animal and human) vie for shelf space with exotic shells and beads.

Soon, the aristocracy of Europe followed Worm's lead. Every educated gentleman had his own "cabinet of curiosities" or *Wunderkammern*, part witch's cave, part scientific laboratory and apothecary's chamber. Even the great artist Rembrandt turned much of his studio into a trove of curiosities.

Between 1688 and 1815, the European naval powers of Spain, the Netherlands, Great Britain and France competed for power and influence, fighting five wars in the process. The empire-builders became just as obsessed with collecting things as they were with dominating new lands. The world's first museums, which would become driving forces in the development of archaeology, were built on the back of "curious" collections like these.

A ROYAL FIRST

The man who must surely count as the world's first archaeologist was the enigmatic Nabû-na'id; also known as Nabonidus, he reigned over Babylon, the most famous city in ancient Mesopotamia, during 556–539 BCE.

Nabonidus ruled a vast empire that stretched from the Persian Gulf to the borders of modern-day Egypt. If he had wanted to succeed as king, he should have spent his time organizing armies, pleasing his people and quashing opposition. Instead, he set off into the desert to

LEFT
The first time capsule? Nabonidus took care to leave a detailed record of his archaeological work, written in cuneiform on this 9-inch (23-cm) clay cylinder, dating from *c.*543 BCE.

uncover and restore archaeological wonders, leaving his feckless son Belshazzar in charge. A remarkable find from the ruins of an ancient temple confirms not just the story of Nabonidus, but also the fate of Belshazzar.

Until the discovery of the Nabonidus Cylinder, no mention of Belshazzar had been found outside of the Book of Daniel in the Bible; as far as official history was concerned, no such person had ever really existed. In 1881, the Assyriologist Hormuzd Rassam discovered a piece of baked clay (a cylinder, now in the Pergamon Museum in Berlin, with a copy in the British Museum) that proved otherwise, in a desert temple. Nabonidus, it transpired, had buried an eloquent record of his existence.

Rassam found the cylinder in ancient Sippar, a cult religious centre whose temple was already more than 2,000 years old when Nabonidus took the throne. Before burying his cylinder, Nabonidus inscribed it with a heartfelt prayer: "As for Belshazzar the eldest son – my offspring – instil reverence for your great godhead in his heart. May he not commit a cultic mistake. May he be sated with a life of plenitude."

Nabonidus describes how, "with the craft of the exorcist", he rediscovered the ancient moon-god temples, and set about restoring them. He repaired at least three temples and a pyramid, as well as preserving King Aššurbanipal's treasure.

Belshazzar allowed Babylon to fall into the hands of the Persians: on 29 October

539 BCE, the city fell to Cyrus the Great, the legendary Persian leader. Belshazzar was almost certainly executed, and Nabonidus was exiled, characterized by the Persians as a lying, uncultured fool.

His fate prefigures a key problem in archaeology: how can one protect places of great antiquity from the forces of destruction? Time has not been kind to Babylon or to ancient Mesopotamia. In recent times, while killing and displacing hundreds of thousands of people,

Flauius Blondus

so-called "Islamic State" (or Daesh) extremists have looted and destroyed many archaeological sites and there has been a systematic cultural and religious cleansing campaign across northern Iraq and Syria.

LESSONS FROM THE PAST

Across the world, interest in the past has waxed and waned. The educated classes of Song Dynasty China (960–1279 CE) believed that the discovery of ancient artefacts could be used in state events. This attitude was criticized, but at the same time it was acknowledged that the objects proved useful by providing information on ancient techniques.

In Renaissance Europe from the 14th century onwards, there was renewed interest in classical culture. Scholars and historians – such as Flavio Biondo (who studied under Ballistario of Cremona and published a series of encyclopaedias) and the artist and architect Leon Battista Alberti – set about documenting the ruins of ancient Rome. In England, the antiquarian and historian William Camden began making a list of monuments as part of a topographical survey he started in 1577. Meanwhile in the Americas, the Spanish had begun to establish rule over vast swathes of land and were discovering the treasures of the indigenous peoples, such as the Maya.

AN APPETITE FOR ADVENTURE

The modern world's first major archaeological expedition began as one big adventure. On the morning of 4 October 1691, a group of 30 men arrived at the ancient city of Palmyra, in the middle of the Syrian desert. Through a fringe of palm trees, an exotic vision of graceful arches, courts and ruined temples rose out of the creamy sands: the home of the legendary King Solomon. At its heart was a great colonnade, a street lined with gracious Corinthian columns.

They had reached one of the most important cultural centres of the ancient world in the 1st–2nd century CE, an opulent caravan oasis. With its place on the Silk Road and intermittently under the rule of Classical Rome, Palmyra had been a cultural powerhouse. Its buildings are strongly original in style, uniting Graeco-Roman art with Persian and even Asian influences.

William Halifax, a one-time chaplain of the Syrian city of Aleppo, admired the extraordinary great Temple of Ba'al. He found a few hundred "miserable people" living among the ruins in dirt shacks, along with their sheikh. "I question somewhat whether any City in the World could have challenged Precedence over this in its Glory," he noted.

The group's report was the first documented account of Palmyra, published by the Royal Society in London

A View of the Ruins of Palmyra alias Tadmor, taken on the

The Temple now inhabited.   Porphyry Pillars.   The Portico   The Se

four years later. It reached a large audience not just in Britain but also in France, the Netherlands and Italy. In it was the first image of Palmyra to reach European eyes: a 180-degree view of the entire city.

The intellectual élite of the West was set afire by the oasis city's stark beauty, kick-starting a frenetic new fashion for Neoclassicism. James Dawkins and Robert Wood travelled there in 1751, gentlemen scholars from the Society of Dilettantes. Their romantic depictions of heroic adventures in the desert inspired the "cult of the sublime" – a Europe-wide love affair with ruins.

This was the first Western contact with Palmyra for hundreds of years, and whetted appetite for more romantic "discoveries"; a story that would end up inspiring travellers like the Swiss explorer Johann Ludwig Burckhardt, who discovered the glorious, isolated ruins of Petra (see page 36) in the Jordanian desert.

Sadly, Palmyra has suffered greatly since Halifax first saw it in the 17th century. Its Arch of Triumph was deliberately destroyed by so-called Islamic State in 2015. Although 3D technology has allowed it to be re-sculpted from Egyptian marble,

using photographs and drawings as a source, this kind of reconstruction is controversial, but shows just how much modern technology can achieve.

An Appetite for Antiquaries: Making History

It was 1707: the first meeting of the British Society of Antiquaries, at the Bear Tavern on the Strand, in the heart of London. It was the world's first such society, and William Stukeley served as its first Secretary.

Fascinated by Stonehenge's solar alignment, he and the renowned astronomer Edmund Halley attempted to date the stones and studied the monument in depth, on site. Their calculations were wrong, but their investigations were nevertheless a key moment in field archaeology. Stukeley's skilled drawings are still used in studies of Stonehenge today (see pages 26–9).

The society that Stukeley helped create tried to get Britain to follow the lead of Sweden, where archaeological sites were already protected by royal statute. It helped establish archaeology's roots in science and observation, and eventually drew up the first UK legislation protecting ancient monuments.

The society also campaigned against the increasing dilapidation of Stonehenge. After Stukeley's time, new housing started to encroach on the monument. An entire trilithon toppled in 1797, and one of the upright sarsens of the outer circle later fell down, along with its lintel. Would this remarkable monument, an icon the world over, survive?

Overseas, meanwhile, other such societies followed the British Antiquaries' example. In India, William Jones founded the Asiatic Society in 1784 and began research into the country's history and other parts of the "Orient". The society eventually handed over its collections to the Indian Museum, which was established in 1814.

ABOVE TOP
Standing on a crossroads between cultures: the beauties of Syria's Palmyra, even in ruined state, took 18th-century visitors by surprise. It continued to delight until it fell prey to war and destruction in the early 21st century.

ABOVE
The multi-talented William Stukeley, antiquarian writer and influential campaigner.

A New Dawn?

In the early 1770s, Thomas Jefferson, the principal author of the US Declaration of Independence, began what was probably the very first modern-style archaeological excavation, to test the accuracy of a theory.

Jefferson decided to examine a mysterious earthwork near his home Monticello, one of a cluster of 13 huge mounds in Virginia's Shenandoah Valley. It was known locally as

RIGHT
Founding father Thomas Jefferson (1743–1826), quite possibly the first real archaeologist.

BELOW
In North America, mounds were built from the Archaic period to the Woodland era and the time of European contact. The most innocuous-looking can hide fascinating secrets of the past or carry symbolic significance for local people, and may appear quite different from far-off compared with close-to.

Monasukapanough. John Smith, the English leader of the Jamestown Virginia colony, had named the area Monacan Indian territory. The indigenous peoples called it *Amai Amañuhkañ*, the "Country of the People of the Land". By this time, however, Virginia's native tribes had all but melted into the landscape.

The settlers found the landscape dotted with enigmatic mounds, some huge, often built in symbolic animal or snake-like shapes that Native Americans were not considered "civilized" enough to have built.

It was argued the builders must have been a "lost race" – variously claimed to be the Vikings, Phoenicians, Tartars, Chinese, Welsh or even the "lost tribes of Israel". Jefferson believed otherwise. When he was eight years old, he had seen a group of Indians approach the mound with what he took to be sorrow. They knew precisely the location of the monument, and how to

Spirit in the Sky

It's a little-known fact that Stonehenge was put up for auction in 1915. Sir Cecil Chubb bought it for £6,600 and gave it to a relieved nation. Visitor damage led to a car park being built at a distance from the henge. Unwittingly, the tarmac was laid on top of ancient wooden post-holes that have recently been carbon dated to about 6,000 years BCE – twice the age of any part of the main henge – and which are now believed to be the very first monumental structures erected in the British Isles.

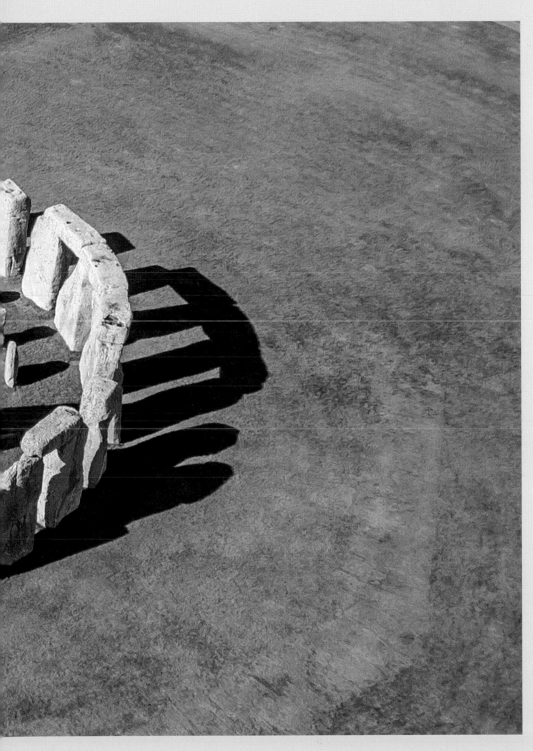

The Structure

When they were first erected 4,600 years ago, the monument's vast, cut-stone sarsens would have glistened a pure, bright white. The chalk barrows and the stately ceremonial Avenue leading down to the River Avon would have shone like marble. The surrounding plain, about seven times the size of New York's Central Park, was grazed by powerful, 1.5-ton/tonne bison-like creatures, wild aurochs.

Why Stonehenge was constructed, and how, has long been a source of speculation and debate. Now, new technology is completely reshaping our understanding. The Stonehenge Hidden Landscapes Project is the world's biggest-ever "virtual" excavation to date. In five years (beginning in 2010), without excavating a thing, it created a digitized body of knowledge that would have taken decades of manual work to create.

The project has revealed up to 20 buried structures that no one has known about until now, including an extraordinary 108-ft (33-m)-long communal burial chamber dating from *c.*4000 BCE. Thanks to this new work, archaeologists now believe that, far from being an isolated structure, this special site on Salisbury Plain formed part of a vast complex of henges, barrows and other features, all spiritually interconnected within a sacred landscape.

LEFT
Stonehenge, that most enigmatic of monuments, casts its shadows over Salisbury Plain in Wiltshire.

ROCKS OF AGES

THE HENGE'S FIRST BEGINNINGS

One of the most exciting results of the digital survey is the previously misunderstood connection it reveals between Stonehenge and the Greater Cursus. This is an immense loop-shaped enclosure more than 1½ miles (2.5 km) long that lies north of the stones. William Stukeley imagined teams of Romans or ancient Britons racing chariots down its length, which is why he gave the feature the Latin name for a racecourse.

The Hidden Landscapes Project found two deep pits at either end of the Cursus, which probably held posts or beacons. Observed from the spot that would later become Stonehenge, the pit on the eastern side aligns with the rising sun on Midsummer's Day. The western pit aligns with its very last blink, at sunset. Stonehenge would be erected, 400 years later, at the exact point where those twin alignments intersect.

Menyn in the Preseli Hills in Wales a full 186 miles (300 km) to the west remains a matter of some debate.

The excavation in the 21st century of a nearby 2,500-year-old hill fort that was occupied in Stonehenge's later heyday led to a new analysis of a spring in the area, Blick Mead. Archaeologists had always believed the feature was part of a relatively modern 18th-century landscape garden. But a rare type of

algae, *Hildenbrandia rivularis*, flourishes at Blick Mead. If you plunge a stone into the waters, expose it to the air and wait a few hours, the algae turn the stone a vivid magenta pink. Did the hunter-gatherers who first noticed the phenomenon believe there was magic at work?

New discoveries such as these all point to Stonehenge being a vibrant international centre or meeting place of some kind. Ground-penetrating radar shows that the area now known as Durrington Walls once held up to 90 standing stones and was the world's largest "super henge", some 1,640 ft (500 m) wide. Furthermore, houses in a

ABOVE
Rare algae found at a spring in the Stonehenge area have magical-seeming properties.

BELOW
The "Amesbury Archer": a fabulously wealthy traveller from *c.*2400–2200 BCE, found buried when a school was built near Stonehenge.

CONSTRUCTION

Stonehenge was built in three broad phases. The first ring ditch was dug *c.*5,000 years ago (i.e. *c.*3000 BCE) at "the dawn" of the Neolithic. Then, around 2500 BCE, huge sarsen stones were brought to the site from the Marlborough Downs many miles away and erected in a precise geometric pattern.

The inner ring of bluestones was added between 100 and 300 years later, forming a rough horseshoe inside the larger ring of sarsen stones. How these "blue" monoliths were moved from near Carn

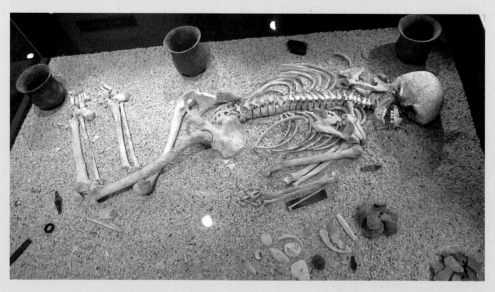

nearby excavation appear to have been inhabited for about 50–100 years around 2500 BCE, at exactly the same time as the huge sarsen stones were being erected.

The Commercial Traveller

From its origins as a spiritual axis for ancient Britons, Stonehenge seems to have transformed into a cultural or spiritual focal point for European peoples. By the beginning of the early Bronze Age, the archaeological evidence suggests it had become a major international centre for trade that drew important and influential visitors from far and wide.

One such visitor would have been the exotic "Amesbury Archer", who lived sometime between 2400 and 2200 BCE. He takes his name from an arrowhead and two sandstone bowstring wrist guards that were found with his skeleton. A pair of gold hair ornaments also with him came from the Mediterranean. Oxygen isotope analysis of his tooth enamel reveals that he grew up in the Alps.

Temple to the ancestors? Place of healing? Astrological observatory? Trading hub? Stonehenge may be one of the most studied prehistoric places in the world, but its full story becomes more complex the more we learn. What is certain is that Stonehenge is one of the richest archaeological landscapes in the world.

HENGE

The "henge" seems to be a purely British phenomenon, except for possibly the "roundel" enclosures of Bavaria's Isar Valley and Kothingeichendorf, which both have causeways very like the Avenue. These are usually found in groups, even if sometimes separated by hundreds of miles. Scholars think they were meeting places, possibly used for ritualistic purposes. In mainland Europe, there are many wooden circles of a much older date, such as the Goseck circle in central Germany, constructed c.4900 BCE.

BELOW
The structural achievement of Stonehenge continues to astound and, despite a rapidly increasing wealth of data, is still far from demystified.

find their way through the woods. Linking the tribesmen in this way was a significant insight, because it contradicted the "lost race" theory.

The 16th-century Spanish explorer Hernando de Soto had wondered if the flat-topped mounds could be the bases of temples. Remembering what he had seen, Jefferson, a formidable personality with opinions to match, was sure they were Native American monuments that had been built for ceremonial purposes.

Jefferson was the first to specify and then test an archaeological hypothesis, seeking answers to specific questions. Crucially, he wanted to know if the "Indian Grave" was a ceremonial burial site, where Indians re-buried their dead standing up, as he believed. He also wondered if the burials could have taken place over hundreds of years. He used two excavation strategies: trenching, which let him see the mound's internal structure, and stratigraphy, a method that put the American founding father about 100 years ahead of his time.

"I first dug superficially in several parts of it, and came to collections of human bones… These were lying in the utmost confusion, some vertical, some oblique, some horizontal, and directed to every point of the compass," he wrote in a painstaking record of his results. We now know that the mounds mostly date back to the late prehistoric and "early contact" era (c.900–1700 CE).

Meanwhile, the Indian story moved west, following the ever-expanding frontier. In 1935, gold diggers became grave robbers when a group of miners blew up the largest of eastern Oklahoma's Spiro Mounds with gunpowder. They found – and sold – so many artefacts that the site became known as the "King Tut of the West".

An Emperor in Egypt

Why do there seem to be at least as many mummies in France as there are in Egypt? Sitting in the Louvre Museum in Paris is an entire "Temple Room", as well as a "Sarcophagus Room". The museum holds works of Egyptian art including the wonderful Crypt of the Sphinx, the Zodiac of Dendera and the famous

Tod treasure, unearthed from a village near Luxor. Meanwhile, in London, the British Museum holds the Rosetta Stone and the incredible monumental sculpture of Ramesses II. Between them, the two institutions possess thousands of magnificent, truly priceless works of Egyptian art as well as smaller items. The collections in London and Paris are a legacy of the long and bitter power struggle between the British and the French. In the 19th century, the two dominant imperial powers fought over the world's cultural capital, filling up their museums as they went. Statue by statue, tomb by tomb, the rivals engaged in a huge game of archaeological one-upmanship. It was a novel way to wage war. Other countries, such as Germany and Austria, weren't far behind, while the Italian Charles Emmanuel III of Turin had already looted 300 items from the Karnak area.

Having led the French into Italy with ease and made Venice "Europe's drawing room", Napoléon Bonaparte was the talk of Europe. He decided to strike England a fatal blow by stabbing at the soft underbelly of the British Empire, seizing control of the land trade route to India. Egypt would be the blade.

On 19 May 1798, Bonaparte sailed from Italy with an army of nearly 54,000 men. With them was another, smaller army of scientists, engineers, artists and linguists – their task to capture not Egyptian soil but Egyptian culture. Napoléon called them his *Savants*, or "Wise Men". It was the world's first large-scale scientific expedition.

The French landed on 2 July and came upon Cairo, a vision from *A Thousand and One Nights*. Between them and their glittering goal was an army of Mameluke soldiers, mounted on noble Arab horses and armed with silver-hilted, curved

OPPOSITE
Inscrutable: French Egyptologist Mariette took control of the antiquities market, transporting the 26-tonne Sphinx of Tanis to Paris in 1825. Now in the Louvre, it dates back to 2600 BCE.

ABOVE
Egypt's finest: the mysterious temple complex at Karnak in Upper Egypt was dedicated to Amun-Ra. For a wealth of information about the vast site, vist UCLA's "Digital Karnak Project".

yataghan sabres. The Ottomans had ruled in Egypt for more than 500 years, supported by this ferocious warrior élite class. Before the ensuing battle, Napoléon famously gestured at the stern geometry of the pyramids and the Horizon of Khufu looming 467 ft (142 m) behind them. "Soldiers," he said, "forty centuries are looking down on you!" The French won the day.

When the Emperor's army came upon the ancient city of Thebes, with its remarkable temples, an *emotion électrique* ran through the soldiers, who burst into spontaneous applause. By August they had taken most of Upper Egypt. Ultimately, though, it was the *Savants* who claimed the greater victory. While the men suffered, the *Savants* explored. They mapped, drew, measured and surveyed.

Artist Dominique-Vivant Denon was the first to draw the temples and ruins at Thebes, Esna, Edfu and Philae. His book of meticulously drawn engravings, which went into 40 editions, set off a wave of Egypt-mania in Europe. Ancient Greece and Rome had always been seen as the definitive prototypes of Western civilization. Now there was an alternative. This was the beginning of an entire

by the occupying Ottoman Turks. In 1812, Elgin transported the sculptures to Britain, skirting bankruptcy in the process; his actions ensured that the Elgin Marbles suffered no further damage in the Greek War of Independence.

branch of archaeology, with its own special name, Egyptology.

As Napoléon's army plundered Egypt, a man named Thomas Bruce, Lord Elgin, hadn't forgotten Greece and Greek art. Britain's ambassador to Constantinople, Elgin bought a permit and removed what was left of the marble frieze on the Parthenon in Athens. Sections of it had been ground up and used as mortar

A FETISH FOR PHAROAHS

In the Anglo–French rivalry for empire, India and Egypt were the key prizes. In 1816, Henry Salt arrived in Egypt as British Consul General. For Salt, this was an opportunity to make money: lots of it. Bernardino Drovetti, an Italian who had served under Napoléon, was his opposite

OPPOSITE
Napoléon Bonaparte in Egypt Viewing an Egyptian Mummy, a painting by Maurice Orange, featuring the *Savants* along with the General.

ABOVE
Vivant Denon's watercolour of *The Obelisk of Cleopatra*. Denon brought Egypt-mania to Paris, and thence to the world.

FOLLOWING PAGES
Some of the Elgin Marbles, minus a number of limbs but still more or less intact, in the British Museum. The possibility of their return to Athens is an ongoing sensitive issue between Britain and Greece.

number in the French camp. With untold riches at stake, archaeology was about to become a whole new battlefield.

Egypt was thick with adventurers, rogues and mavericks who could scent a fortune in the sands. Enthusiastic and scholarly collectors like the wealthy dilettante Sir William Bankes, intent on bagging an obelisk for his English country garden, were also on the prowl. The cast of characters included the Swiss explorer Johann Ludwig Burckhardt, fresh from two years travelling in disguise as "The Sheikh" Ibrahim ibn Abdallah. Burckhardt had made expeditions to Palmyra, Damascus and Baalbek and into the untamed lands of Hauran in Syria/ Jordan. He had also made two sensational discoveries: the first was the abandoned Nabatean city of Petra in Jordan, and the second was the great sand-swept temple at Abu Simbel, in Nubia in southern Egypt. Burckhardt fell in with a strange Italian

from Padua, a water engineer who was on his uppers. It was Burckhardt who would introduce the "Great Belzoni" to Salt. Thus began the "War of the Consuls".

Egypt's ruthless ruler Pasha Muhammad Ali was struggling to establish the country as a modern nation. He was quite happy to exchange the past for the present. Ali cunningly played the consuls of the world's two most dangerous and predatory nations off against each other for Egyptian gain.

Belzoni was the most unlikely Egyptologist in the world, but Burckhardt saw beneath the surface: this was a very determined man with a range of rare skills, particularly when it came to engineering. Belzoni delighted in the explorer's stories, one of which concerned the head of the "Young Memnon", which lay separated from its colossal body in the burning sands on the west bank of the Nile. It was an effigy of "Ozymandias",

ABOVE
The famous explorer Johann Burckhardt, who became fluent in Arabic and spent years venturing into the desert in disguise.

BELOW
The remarkable hidden enclave of Petra in the Jordanian desert. Burckhardt's were the first Western eyes to see it.

the Greek name for Ramesses II, and the inspiration behind Shelley's sonnet.

Armed with Burckhardt's information, Belzoni rampaged around Egypt, trying to stay one step ahead of Drovetti and his sidekick, the military deserter Jean-Jacques Rifaud. The French had been granted a licence to excavate at Thebes, and the remarkable complex at Karnak that the Egyptians knew as Ipet Issu ("the most select of places") – a fact that infuriated Salt, who knew that they had stolen a march on him.

Burckhardt and Belzoni persuaded Salt that the "Young Memnon", stuck in the desert near Thebes, should be resurrected and given to the British Museum. Napoleon's army had already tried to move the statue, using gunpowder "to blow off its wig", and found it an impossible task.

Unfortunately for Belzoni, Drovetti was one step ahead of him. When he asked the local Bey for permission to remove the statue, Drovetti arrived in person. He told Belzoni that no labour would be made available to help in the enormous task. Undeterred and ever-resourceful, Belzoni realized that the best way to move the statue was to use the Nile's waters. He also realized that there was a ticking clock: the great river would flood in a month's time.

FOLLOWING PAGES
No easy task: the "Great Belzoni" and his workmen haul away at the "Young Memnon".

GIOVANNI BATTISTA BELZONI (1778–1823)

Born in Padua, the son of a barber, Belzoni had a varied career, first studying hydraulics before working as a barber in the Netherlands. A meeting in Malta with Ismael Gibraltar, an emissary of Muhammad Ali, the Khedive of Egypt, took him to Egypt where, on the recommendation of Johann Burckhardt, he began work for Henry Salt. He is most noted for his work at the Ramesseum at Thebes, the great temple at Edfu and Abu Simbel and Karnak.

The race was on. Belzoni found the statue and proceeded to hire 80 labourers of his own. With 14 wooden poles, four palm-leaf ropes and four sledge rollers, he set about moving Ozymandias.

He often worked at night avoiding the daytime heat: he levered rollers underneath the statue front and back. Some dragged, some pulled; no doubt Belzoni added his great strength. Then everyone hauled the pink granite statue inch by inch towards the river, moving the back roller to the front as they progressed.

After a month of waiting for Salt's promised boat to turn up, Rifaud arrived aboard a large boat bound for Aswan. He refused Belzoni use of the boat. Every day, the Nile was getting lower, and even Belzoni's bribes had ceased to have any effect on the locals: he could not get out of Thebes. Until Drovetti made the mistake of presenting another local dignitary, the Casheff of Erments, with a jar of sardines. The Casheff was outraged by such a pathetic gift. Heaping Belzoni with lavish praise, he invited the strongman and his English wife, Sarah, to a feast. The Great Belzoni would get all the help he wanted, could take any boat he wanted – any statues, for that matter. Never one to turn down an opportunity, Belzoni grabbed a few statues from Karnak for good measure, built a mud ramp down to the Nile – where for one heart-stopping moment the "Young Memnon" sank into the mud – and set off with Sarah for Cairo.

Belzoni had caught the bug. Using methods that would make a modern archaeologist scream – he thought nothing of opening sealed tombs with a battering ram – he plundered everything of value in sight. He dug through 20 ft (6 m) of hardened sand to get at the monuments of Abu Simbel, rediscovered the entrance to the Great Pyramid and found five tombs in the Valley of the Kings, including that of Seti I, thereby paving the way for a long series of important excavations that others could now undertake.

In 1844, the American vice-consul, George Gliddon, made an emotional appeal. All this pillaging had to stop: "Words cannot express our rage… about all the demolition that has taken place here [at Karnak]."

Fortunately, there were signs of a new, more thoughtful approach developing among individuals who would approach Egypt's majestic past with greater respect. The new cast included a French artist named Frédéric Cailliaud, who would diligently copy hundreds of ancient documents and papyri. William Bankes also copied thousands of inscriptions, *in situ*, including the name of Ramesses II. The efforts of these two men, one French and one English, eventually helped a young man called Champollion to decipher the Rosetta Stone.

Pompeii, which had begun in the mid 1700s (see pages 42–5), had become a significant tourist destination. Democratic ideals were the silent symbolism behind many of the new public buildings in France, Britain and the fledgling USA. Winckelmann added to that the notion that a society's civil success was pinned to the quality, or "nobility", of its art. The evolution of art, he argued, paralleled the life cycle of civilizations.

Pro-Greek sentiment was exploding across Europe, fuelled by accounts of atrocities committed by the occupying Ottomans. The British colonel Martin William Leake was sent on a spying mission: he brought back booty which is now mainly in the Fitzwilliam Museum, in Cambridge.

In 1811, as Elgin was busily transporting the Acropolis's marbles across the Mediterranean, a group of amateur archaeologists forged a multicultural friendship that would finally put the archaeology first. The German architects Jacob Linkh, Otto Magnus von Stackelberg and Carl von Hallerstein met English counterparts John Foster and Charles Robert Cockerell in Athens. Rome had long been part of the Grand Tour, a kind of open-air finishing school for rich young gentlemen, but now Athens, too, was *de rigueur*. The group made drawings at the Acropolis, in Sounion and on

the island of Aegina, where Hallerstein excavated at the Temple and the Jupiter Panhellenion. Although Hallerstein removed some of the remains to the Glyptothek in Munich, the group had done valuable work in documenting and publicizing important ancient Greek sites. They consolidated the work of the 18th-century architectural historians Stuart and Revett, and cemented the long archaeological love affair between the Prussians, the English and Greece.

With admirable clarity of ambition, the German government funded a scientific expedition to Olympia directed by a young historian, Ernst Curtius. In a world first, it was agreed that artefacts were to remain in Greece, according to contracts drawn up between the Greek and German governments. Curtius was given the support of the best German archaeologists of the period, including Friedrich Adler and Wilhelm Dorpfeld.

OPPOSITE
Antiquary Charles Townley and friends at his house in Westminster, painted by Johann Zoffany in 1782. In the foreground is the famous "Disc-thrower" by Greek sculptor Myron, a technical marvel. Townley's extensive collection eventually went to the British Museum.

BELOW
Athens's magnificent Parthenon temple, standing on the rocky outcrop of the Acropolis. To visitors in the 18th and 19th centuries this building seemed to epitomize spirituality and unity, but in fact it was once a riot of colour, not the pared-down structure seen today. Teams of international excavators have competed to work here.

GREECE AND THE DEMOCRATIC IDEAL

Together, the pen and the sword galvanized the first ever formal excavations in Greece.

When Johann Joachim Winckelmann wrote his influential *History of the Art of Antiquity* he portrayed Classical – mainly Greek – art as the pinnacle of European civilization. The German cobbler's son was riding a wave of intellectual curiosity fed by Greece's isolation under Ottoman rule.

To European societies, the Classical civilizations of Greece and Rome embodied the best of civic and artistic virtues. Indeed, the excavations of

WHERE TIME STOPPED

It was 24 August 79 CE, a seemingly normal day in Pompeii in the Bay of Naples. Shortly after midday, a cracking noise split the summer air, and a menacing dark plume began to rise from the summit of nearby Mount Vesuvius. At first onlookers merely wondered at it. Then surprise turned to terror and shock. Vesuvius began shooting ash, stones and deadly fumes into the sky.

Day turned to night. Around 300 people tried to escape from the shore. Their bodies were carbonized where they stood, cowered or knelt. Fifteen miles (24 km) away, the Roman author Pliny and his family watched the disaster unfold across the bay.

In a rich seaside resort 10 miles (16 km) to the west, the catastrophe hit even harder. In Herculaneum, cascades of scorching ash and toxic gases (known as pyroclastic surges) brought the residents almost instant death. An entire world was snuffed out in a matter of minutes.

In Herculaneum, the heat actually carbonized organic substances like food, wood or leather, preserved for us to see.

ABOVE
Painted some 50 years before Pompeii's eruption, the "Villa of the Mysteries" fresco is thought to show the initiation of a young woman into a mystery cult. The villa is about ¼ mile (400 m) north of Pompeii, and may have belonged to a wealthy freedman, Istacidius Zosimus.

At Pompeii, it was different. Objects and people alike were encased in ash and lava that later hardened to a porous shell. Around 38 per cent of those who tried to flee were killed by falling roofs and collapsing walls. Two relatively ordinary places were rendered extraordinary, because of their sudden and terrible fate. Old loaves of bread sit in the oven. A mosaic "Beware of the Dog" sign is still visible in an entranceway, as are the political slogans for the upcoming elections.

Now the world's oldest archaeological site, it was one of the first ever to be excavated. What does it tell us? At Pompeii, in particular, life does appear to have been full of vice, at least by Victorian standards. Slavery was an accepted aspect of the daily lives of the Romans. Estimates vary, but it is thought that roughly one in three of those who lived in Italy at the time was enslaved.

However, there were also many genial aspects to life in Pompeii, not least the sumptuous fountains in the crowded streets and a well-fed way of life that was, ironically enough, helped by the fecundity of the local volcanic soil. Up until the moment of destruction, Pompeii was prosperous, and growing.

Footprints found embedded in a terracotta tile atop a temple roof demonstrate an unexpected bilingual friendship. Detfri and Amica worked in a tile factory, and perhaps did the roofing together as well. The Oscan native language works from right to left (despite being local to southern Italy). Written into the tile are the words: "Detfri, slave of Herennius Sattius, signed with a footprint." Then Amica joins her friend, writing in Latin, left to right: "Amica, slave of Herennius. Signed when we were placing the tile."

To modern archaeologists and historians, this otherwise everyday moment shows an empire still in transition. Within a century, the Oscan language would completely disappear, swallowed up by Latin. It is insights like these that make Pompeii and its archaeological legacy unique.

People in Plaster

The 19th-century Italian excavator Giuseppe Fiorelli noticed four cavities in the layers of solidified ash in Pompeii. He realized that if he poured plaster of Paris into these voids, he could create positive copies. The first time he did this, he revealed four poignant figures: a man carrying a bag of money was leading his two small daughters, the youngest with her hair braided. Scrambling through the rubble behind them, his wife clutches a medallion of the goddess of luck.

Pompeii's cast figures are unnerving – a haunting memorial to human suffering. People are immortalized exactly as they died: a soldier who is trying to run with his long sword, a stabbing dagger and a bag of tools… A baby left in the crib in the House of the Mosaic Atrium… A man holding an axe, with which he had

tried to break through a door. Perhaps the best-known cast is of a dog, fixed forever in the moment of its terror, trying to bite off its tail.

Archaeology Gets Real

Guiseppe Fiorelli directed the Pompeii excavation from 1863 to 1875 – and hit on a better way to preserve its ruins. Before him, most of the buildings had been excavated from the side. The result was often the destruction of supporting walls and other valuable evidence. Fiorelli began uncovering the houses from the top down.

Like other archaeologists working from this period onward, he sought to employ scientific methods. Work was conducted in a systematic way, with the entire site

RIGHT
Plaster cast of a dog, caught in the throes of death.

EXCAVATION TIMELINE

1709
Theatre at Herculaneum found when a well is dug out

1735
Charles of Bourbon sends Marcello Venuti to investigate

1748
Excavations begin at Pompeii: Karl Weber develops new recording system

1860
Giuseppe Fiorelli introduces new methods

1911
Vittorio Spinazzola uses photography to record the stages of his excavation

divided into a numbered classification system of "regions", *insulae* (blocks) and *domus* (houses). He approached new areas according to a plan, rather than randomly searching for treasure. His numbering system exists in Pompeii to this day, and his methods were not just extremely influential but, in archaeological terms, invaluable.

His work showed that after the eruption, some of the luckier inhabitants actually came back: "This room has already been gone through," reads a scrawled graffito on one of Pompeii's uppermost walls.

The twin towns were entirely forgotten for more than 1,500 years. Pliny (the Younger) lost his uncle that day, and left us the only written account.

Archaeology has given the people of Pliny's time new life. One of the brightest, most delightful works of art ever found came to light only in the 1970s, in the House of the Golden Bracelet near Herculaneum. The fresco shows a glorious half-wild garden, decorated with sculptures and fountains. In it flutter beautiful wild birds: a shy golden oriole, a jay, a swallow, a magpie. It's exciting to think that there may still be many such heart-stopping frescoes waiting to be excavated.

OPPOSITE
Detail from the garden fresco, in the "House of the Golden Bracelet", Herculaneum.

ABOVE RIGHT
Sixth-century BCE mosaic over a fountain in the "House of Neptune and Amphritite", Herculaneum.

MOSAICS

Mosaic floors were made of thousands of small cubes of stone, glass or marble called *tesserae*. These were laid on a bed of mortar and then flattened with a wooden plank or tray to make the surface even. The *tesserae* were then grouted with mortar and "waxed" with a coating of olive oil. The oil enhanced the colours, as well as protecting the mosaic. Mosaics with pictorial scenes were made with the tiniest tesserae, sometimes smaller than a square centimetre. This fineness meant that the artist could vary colour, shade and line in very delicate detail. The technique is called *opus vermiculatem*, (literally "wormlike work"). The actual scene, usually set in the centre, was known as the *emblema*. Some of the world's best and biggest mosaic floors are from Pompeii, including *The Battle of Issus*, which shows Alexander the Great in battle. It is made with more than 4 million individual *tesserae*.

Six years later, most of the buildings reported by Pausanias had been cleared and identified, including the Heraion, the Temple of Zeus, the Metroon, the Philippeion, the precinct of Pelops and the Echo Colonnade. With its own national identity, Greece could now enact its own laws. It would no longer be possible to simply come and remove the great treasures of Hellenic culture without so much as a protest. There would still be some figures, though, who would try, including one spectacularly unscrupulous adventurer: Heinrich Schliemann.

THE SIEGE OF TROY

Heinrich Schliemann had decided to devote his life to a great mystery: the *Iliad*, Homer's epic poem about the kidnapping of the beautiful Helen and the ten-year siege of Troy. Was Troy a real city, and if so, could it be found?

In 1858, at the age of 36 and wealthy due to trading in gold dust, Schliemann was rich beyond dreams. He met Frank Calvert, a quiet and unassuming diplomat who was an expert on Homer. For 20 years, Calvert had studied the "Troad", near the Dardenelles, drawing sites, comparing records and trying to convince the British Museum to fund excavations. He believed that he had found the legendary site of Troy within a prominent "tell", or mound, at Hissarlik. The Persian ruler Xerxes, Alexander the Great Ottoman and Sultan Mehmed II had all recognized this as the site of Troy. Calvert's trial trenches suggested that the site had twice been burned to the ground, fitting with Homer's account.

ABOVE
The Temple of Olympian Zeus in Athens, a colossal structure that symbolizes the fractious meetings of Greece and Rome. It was begun in 520 BCE, but finished much later in the Corinthian style by a Roman architect. Its glory was short-lived: it was sacked in Sulla's 87–86 BCE siege of Athens.

LEFT
Ernst Curtius, said to have invented the concept of a "big dig". He also brought a new collaborative spirit to excavation, arranging for artefacts found at Olympia to stay in Greece. He is also said to have brought a new rigour into archaeology.

Scenting an opportunity for fame, Schliemann became officially enamoured with the legend of Troy, claiming it had been a boyhood obsession. He quickly became the Englishman's business partner – and then took over.

Schliemann's first finds were modest, made under the watchful eye of a Turkish official, Amin Effendi: clay cups and bowls decorated with owls, the goddess Athena's sacred motif. Schliemann had ordered all real owls in the area to be shot, because he hated their cries ringing through the cabin at night.

His diaries show his lack of experience, and how confused he was by what he saw in the trenches he cut. He hadn't realized how much hard work excavating was. To his relief, he eventually found a wall, which he declared to be the "Sacred Tower of Ilium".

"Everyone must now admit," he wrote, "that I have solved a great historical puzzle." He began sending his letters from "Troy".

Schliemann's professional bacon was saved when a young Wilhelm Dörpfeld, a pioneer of stratigraphic excavation, came to him fresh from Ernst Curtius's excavations at Olympia. Like Schliemann, Dörpfeld was also obsessed with proving the truth behind Homer's epics, but his ordered and methodical approach made him much the better archaeologist.

Schliemann was prone to smuggling his finds out of the country. One early May morning, he saw the gleam of gold and copper in the ground – and declared that his workers should take *paidos*, a rest break. The find included a golden cup, with the handles of a ship, decorated earrings, gold rings and bracelets, silver plus an elaborate diadem – a headdress made of 16,000 golden pieces – much of which became known as the "Jewels of Helen". He hid the treasures in his second wife Sophia's shawl, and the couple set off hot-foot to his on-site house. Overnight, fearing discovery, they moved the loot

ABOVE TOP
Little remains of the glory of Troy, but new excavations in the surrounding area are revealing much about the scale of this Bronze Age powerhouse.

ABOVE
Heinrich Schliemann's huge fortune meant that he had no need to raise funds to excavate. He could afford to just plough on and on...

to a nearby farmhouse. Schliemann's diary entry claims that he was saving the treasure for Greece and "for archaeology". Then he promptly made off with it. The Turks, who still owned half of the site, were not pleased.

Schliemann never let the truth get in the way of a good story. He photographed Sophia in the "Jewels of Helen", and then announced that "the great Schliemann has discovered Troy!"

Or had he? Schliemann appears to have been lying. His diaries are heavily doctored. Sophia wasn't even present at the time he found "Priam's treasure" – she was in Athens, because her father was sick. A *Times* newspaper editorial even suggested that the showman had faked the jewellery and had placed it in the ground himself.

In the wet winter of 1876, Schliemann set off again, having been banned from the Turkish empire. He'd written to the Greek authorities, asking to excavate at Olympia and Mycenae, convinced that the latter was the home of the great warrior king Agamemnon. Wisely, the Greeks refused him permission.

Undaunted, Sophia and Schliemann duly turned up at Mycenae, telling the local authorities that they had a government permit. He hired a team of workers who dug for 20 days in the steaming heat before they were nearly arrested. Then the Turks stepped in. They were taking Schliemann to court for the disappearance of "Priam's treasure".

Still, Schliemann had more than enough money to get himself out of trouble. He finally got the go-ahead to excavate at Mycenae in 1876, although the Greek Archaeological Society kept a strict eye on him. Within a month, the team had uncovered the first of several Bronze Age chieftains. They were each buried in a "Cyclopean" tomb with spectacular weapons, wearing extraordinary gold funerary masks. This time, unable to abscond with the lot, Schliemann had to make do with the publicity. Modest as always, he announced that he had found the tombs of Agamemnon, Cassandra and Eurymedon….

Schliemann's methods were destructive and his antics illegal. Nevertheless, his dauntless spirit and compulsive storytelling inspired a whole generation to take up archaeology.

Most experts these days agree that the mound at Hissarlik was indeed Troy. Yet Schliemann's real legacy is unveiling another civilization altogether, one that we scarcely understood existed. That society was not Homeric, but Mycenaean. Schliemann and those who followed him gave us proof that advanced civilizations existed in the long-distant past during the Bronze Age.

In the 1980s, US Professor Manfred Korfmann revealed that there was a wider city of Troy. It had once extended much further out on to the plain. He also found proof in the citadel of a battle that took place in the 12th century BCE. Turkish archaeologists are still excavating the area today.

LEFT
Sophia Schliemann in the "Jewels of Helen". Some accused her husband of having the headdress made up in the local market.

BELOW
Schliemann found the fragments of this bowl on the acropolis of Mycenae and dubbed it the "Warrior Vase" because of its depictions of soldiers.

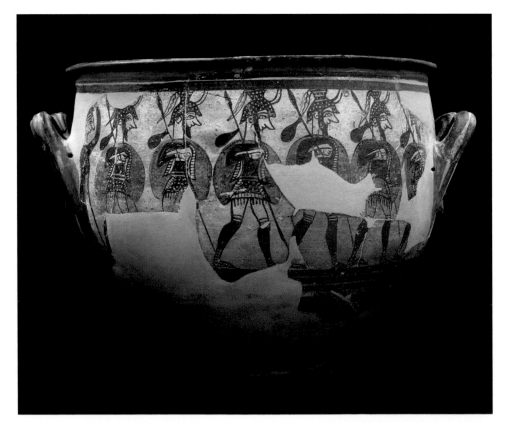

THE LIGHT OF KNOWLEDGE

The wave of romantic nationalism that had swept Europe gave new, explosive impetus to the ideal of garnering fresh knowledge. Helped of course by a new and enlarged understanding about "deep time" and the true breadth of human history (see page 86), which had been turned on their head by the theories of Darwin, archaeology began to develop a new academic rigour.

The work that had begun with small groups of amateur scholars like Stukeley, fascinated by Stonehenge, or Boucher de Perthes, obsessed with documenting the tools used by ancient man, was about to be put on a professional footing. Gradually, the practice of rich men funding their own excavations or poor men attempting to make their fortunes through treasure hunting was subsiding, as a combination of private philanthropic societies and nation states stepped in.

Sweden had appointed a chair for archaeology in the 17th century; now Leiden University in Holland appointed the world's first archaeology professor, Caspar Reuvens. In Denmark, Jens Worsaae began the fight against the "historical theory" of mythology, which held that the Old Norse myths were literally true. He argued that prehistory

was a period best studied not by historians but by archaeologists, dealing with hard, material evidence, and took the Thomsen Three-Age system out into fieldwork. His layer-by-layer excavation style gradually became the standard throughout Europe – a major example of its earliest use was the excavation of Pompeii (see pages 42–5).

Inspired by the remarkable achievements of Champollion in decoding the Rosetta Stone (see page 106) archaeology was, inch by inch, becoming a field of highly qualified specialists, whose methods were strikingly more methodical than their predecessors'. The pioneers included Karl Richard Lepsius who, in 1866, found the Decree of Canopus at Tanis. Written in three languages, the decree proved that Champollion's ground-breaking translation of hieroglyphics had been right.

During his travels in Egypt, Lepsius made extensive maps, plans and drawings of temples that are often the only record left. They were still being used 100 years later in 1980 to identify a "Headless Pyramid" that since Lepsius's day had been covered by a 25-ft (8-m)-high dune of sand. Lepsius, often known as the "Father of Egyptology" (although there are a number of contenders for that title), commissioned the Theinhardt font, the first hieroglyphic typeface.

Augustus Pitt Rivers, whose remarkable anthropological museum in Oxford still delights visitors today, broke the mould by visualizing his work, making it easier to understand with his highly detailed models and plans. He examined many areas of the UK, including his own estate, Cranbourne Chase, in England.

Innovation was the order of the day in Victorian England, as was the drive for "improvement". Sir William Flinders Petrie was part of the first wave of the new professionals. He brought many useful skills that were entirely new to archaeology, including surveying, which he had been taught by his engineer father. Petrie, a brilliant mathematician, managed to refute the widespread idea that there was a "pyramid inch" by

CHARLES DARWIN AND THE ORIGINS OF MAN

Encouraged by the ever more startling evidence from geologists and archaeologists, science was about to rewrite the history of life on earth. Charles Darwin's ideas worried him so much that he confessed his concerns to his future wife, Emma Wedgwood, who urged him to read St John's Gospel. For the next 20 years, Darwin kept his more detailed conclusions to himself. Did the Theory of Evolution prove that human beings were nothing more than intelligent animals? And if humankind was the product of evolution, then what about our moral accountability to God? No less unsettling was the idea that *Homo sapiens* was not a unique creation, but one among several types of early human species. In addition, new scientific theories about glaciation raised the possibility that the Earth had experienced several Ice Ages. Thus, 1859 saw not only the publication of *On the Origin of Species*, but also the Royal Society in London published the results of decades of work by Jacques Boucher de Perthes, documenting the series of prehistoric tools he had found deep in the earth.

LEFT
Danish archaeologist Jens Worsaae, the first to employ stratigraphy.

ABOVE
Some of Jacques Boucher de Perthes' discoveries. Stone tools can help us track *Homo sapiens*'s past life on Earth.

spending two years making a detailed survey of the Great Pyramid at Giza and the surrounding plain. The "inch" theory assumed that the British system of measures came from a divine and ancient source – basically inspired by the ancient Egyptians. His triangulation survey of the pyramid plateau, begun in 1880, was so accurate it is still the foundation of data used today.

Excavation is destructive. Petrie realized just how important were documentation and robust methodology. In future, people would be able to re-interpret his evidence if they needed to – especially given the number of publications he put out. Petrie and his wife Hilda went on to do work in most of Egypt's important sites, devising a new system called sequence dating. This meant adapting the Thomsen method, separation of technology types, and extending it into "typologies". Styles of pottery are used to identify stages in time.

Petrie supervised everything himself. He described Egypt as "a house on fire". Appalled at the rate of destruction he saw, he documented as much as he could, using the archaeologist's favourite new tool: photography.

In the bad old days of Egyptology, there would be a 50:50 split of finds between Egypt and the excavator. From Petrie's time onwards, Egypt, like many other states, insisted that finds remained in the country. This posed a problem in terms of funding. Petrie's private backers, like the Manchester businessman Jesse Haworth, expected a return on their investment.

In the other pervading spirit of the age, a philanthropist intervened: the wealthy novelist Amelia Edwards. Edwards had become a tireless campaigner, trying to stop the destruction and neglect of Egyptian antiquity, following a trip to Abu Simbel in 1873. She co-founded the Egypt Exploration Fund, which raised independent finances for archaeology, and made sure that Petrie got an academic post at University College, London. From then on, Petrie could afford to spend half his time in London, teaching, and the digging season doing fieldwork in Egypt and then Palestine, where he is buried.

Petrie embodies the spirit of the next wave of professional archaeologists, dedicated men and women who travelled far and wide to unpick the tangled skein of world history: Alfred Kidder frantically working out a new chronology that would work for the Americas; Dorothy Garrod's revealing work in the Palaeolithic caves of Mount Carmel; Max Uhle's work in Bolivia, Peru and Chile; and Gertrude Caton Thompsen's challenge to Western assumptions about African culture. Often, their work convinced national

governments to protect their most precious, if then often unrecognized, monuments. Uhle, however, still had to be supported by a rich donor: in this case, it was Phoebe Hearst, the mother of American newspaper magnate William Randolph Hearst. It was not until after World War II that institutional funding became the main commercial lifeline of the archaeologist.

BEHIND THE UNDERGROWTH

In the meantime, another wealthy American was about to take centre stage in the unfolding story. This romantic figure sat squarely within the adventurous tradition with which archaeology had begun, but he was no tomb raider. He also took full advantage of a new 20th-century weapon: mass publicity.

If ever a man deserves the claim to be the "real" Indiana Jones, surely it is American adventurer, aviator and academic Hiram Bingham III. Like his film-screen counterpart, even down to the swashbuckling hat, Bingham was both an

academic (he taught history and politics at Harvard) and a dauntless traveller with a taste for adventure.

In 1911, almost delirious with the altitude, Hiram Bingham found himself high in the jungles of Peru. Below him stretched miles of verdant sub-tropical rainforest, wreathed in mist. Bingham and his small team had pushed up to 7,970 ft (2,430 m) above sea level into the Andes in search of the ruins of the last city of the Inca, Vitcos. Now, with the rapids roaring thousands of feet below, he was threading his way between great granite precipices.

All of a sudden, the American explorer came upon a starkly beautiful, towering terrace of stone, smothered with vines. They had found a lost city, a near-miracle of engineering, a palace complex that stood almost literally on top of the world: Machu Picchu (see pages 54–7).

Word of the "discovery" spread fast across the world, helped by the explorer's extraordinary ability as a publicist. Bingham always carried a camera. Unfortunately, his subsequent excavations and the rumours that surrounded them led to decades of acrimonious rhetoric. At one point in 2008, Peru even filed a lawsuit against Yale University. Finally, the parties came to terms and set up the Museo Machu Picchu at Cuzco, with most of the excavation team's finds now jointly owned.

What of Bingham's skills as an archaeologist? Bingham has had many critics – he had wrongly assumed, for example, that the site was a similar age to archaic Greece. But even now, Machu Picchu's real origins are still, like the great mountain behind it, full of mists. Research continues today.

THE SPIES WHO CAME IN FROM THE DIG

Question: *Who makes the perfect spy?*
Answer: *An archaeologist.*

Archaeologists have a perfect excuse for crossing international borders. They tend to be good at remembering detail, and have legitimate reasons to ask for access to historical archives. They often have natural opportunities to watch troop movements, or note the distribution of military hardware and bases. It would be strange if they didn't ask questions about local culture – and they can often decipher dead languages, a useful skill in mastering codes. No wonder so many archaeologists have worked for the intelligence services.

During World War 1, two young men from the British Museum began to explore and survey the southern frontier of Palestine. One was Leonard Woolley, a stellar figure in 20th-century archaeology, with many credits in the early fight to turn it into a scientific discipline. The other was a young (and

ABOVE
Nahal Me'arot caves at the UNESCO World Heritage site in the Mount Carmel range near Haifa in Israel. This area was excavated by British archaeologist Dorothy Garrod.

THE LOST CITY?

When Bingham first saw Machu Picchu, he took the ancient citadel to be a temple to the sun, given the spiritual atmosphere of the surrounding landscape. He interpreted three unusual windows looking on to the vast mountain ranges beyond as representations of the three caves from which the mythological Inca Children of the Sun had walked into the world.

Bingham surveyed, cleared and excavated the site between 1912 and 1915, thanks to sponsorship by Yale University. *National Geographic* devoted its entire April 1913 issue to Machu Picchu and Hiram Bingham became an all-American – and then global – sensation.

Inevitably, the archaeologist overtook the site to become the story, despite efforts to keep the focus on the citadel. "We are guided solely by love and science," wrote Bingham to the *El Commercio* newspaper, "and the absolute desire to give Peru the fame it deserves."

Amid the media debate, he had his supporters. An editorial in the same newspaper argued: "Yale acts... for the benefit of Peru: it will, at its own expense, bring to life this unknown world, which has been deteriorating under the destructive action of the centuries."

Some argue that the site was a retreat, perhaps even a form of spa, for an Inca élite. Mountain or sun worship does seem a possibility. The "Inti Watana" stone was literally a "hitching post" for the sun – to lasso and keep it in its course. "Inti Mach'ay", a cave where light penetrates only for a few days in December, was the scene of a special ritual where boys watched the sun rise as they were initiated into manhood.

A Slip of the Eye

But was there ever a treasure chest? A full hundred years later, in 2011, a mountain landslide stranded French engineer David Crespy at Machu Picchu. He decided to take a longer look at the site. Not far from the entrance, he noticed an opening blocked by boulders. Crespy recorded thinking, "This is a door." The entrance was standing in plain sight, and had been seen by thousands of visitors.

The tourist reported his hunch to local Peruvian archaeologists, who promised to investigate. More than a year later, they still hadn't done anything. A frustrated Crespy contacted French historian and explorer Thierry Jamin, who had spent many years in Peru. Jamin agreed with Crespy – what lay beyond the boulders might well repay investigation.

On 19 December 2011, Jamin asked the Peruvian Ministry of Culture if his multinational team of experts could survey the space beneath the building. They would use remote-sensing, non-invasive instruments: ground-penetrating radar, an electro-magnetic resonance gun and a molecular frequency discriminator (MFD). Granted official permission, the research project went ahead in March 2012.

Almost at once, the first sensor detected a staircase, two corridors and a square central chamber. They found they could map a 3D picture of the underground complex to a depth of some 65 ft (20 m). The geo-radar also revealed several smaller rooms and a series of cavities that looked as if they might be graves.

The team swept the subterranean complex with the instruments again. The results were even more astonishing. The steps leading down to the central chamber were made of gold. Had they discovered the mausoleum of Pachacutec? The sensors showed there were more gold and silver objects inside.

On 22 May 2012, Jamin asked the Ministry of Culture if he and his team

ABOVE
The soaring terraces of Machu Picchu, now cleared of vines and undergrowth.

RIGHT
The "Inti Watana" or "hitching post", to catch the sun as it passes through the mountains.

could remove the giant boulders blocking access to the subterranean complex and investigate it in person. In November 2012, with local officials criticizing what they described as the project's "lack of scientific methodology", Peru's Directorate General of Cultural Heritage turned him down. The Ministry of Culture and Machu Picchu's directors also said they were worried that any excavation could jeopardize the stability of the site, a concern others dismiss.

One thing is for certain: if the Peruvian authorities ever do allow an archaeological team to investigate and they find the Inca equivalent of King Tut's tomb, then the number of tourists wishing to visit Machu Picchu will explode.

POPULARITY

Machu Picchu's immense popularity is today threatening to overwhelm both it and the local region. The Peruvian authorities have now limited visitor numbers to 2,500 a day. Nevertheless, they allowed the construction of a luxury hotel very close to the entrance. Mass tourism and associated development is undermining the natural habitat of animals like the "Spectacled" or Andean Short-faced bear, the model for the much-loved children's story character Paddington Bear. Archaeological exploration brings wonders to light – but is our desire to visit sites like Machu Picchu in large numbers a good thing?

BELOW
The "Temple of the Moon" lies underneath the overhang of a cave. Different doors are said to symbolize the underworld, the heavens and the Earth. The amazingly fine ashlar stonework has secret doors and panels hidden behind the façade.

HIRAM BINGHAM III (1875–1956)

Tall, lean and handsome, Bingham was lucky enough to marry the granddaughter of the jeweller Charles L. Tiffany, whose wealth was one reason that the academic could afford to travel more or less at whim. Bingham was a Mayflower descendant whose grandfather and great-grandfather, both also named Hiram, were Protestant missionaries.

BELOW
The "Temple of the Sun". Studies in 2013 indicate that Machu Picchu was an integral part of of a complex secret Inca trail through inaccessible high mountain passes.

also bona fide) archaeologist who had graduated from Oxford only four years earlier, Thomas Lawrence. In later life, he became known as "Lawrence of Arabia", one of the 20th century's most brilliant and fascinating military minds, credited with the invention of modern guerrilla warfare.

T. E. Lawrence was a genuine archaeologist, but then he was also a genuine spy. The mission? The so-called "Wilderness of Zin" survey. Concerned that the Ottoman Turks would join the war on the side of the Germans and Austrians, British Intelligence wanted to confirm a route for an army to cross the desert to attack at Suez, a vital strategic link between Britain and its most important colony, India. The desert lands that lay between Palestine and the southern borders of the crumbling Ottoman Empire were virtually uncharted. Lawrence had already walked 1,100 miles (1,770 km) on foot while doing his university thesis, on Crusader castles in Syria, Lebanon and Israel. His particular mission in 1911 was to monitor German progress on a railway linking Berlin with Baghdad.

Their mission sat under the cloak of the Palestine Exploration Fund, a legitimate organization specializing in biblical archaeology that still operates today. Woolley and Lawrence would excavate the site of the biblical Carchemish (Karkemish), once the eastern capital of the ancient Hittite empire, and according to the Bible, the site of the defeat of the Assyrian empire at the

RIGHT
First, learn to ride a camel: Lawrence of Arabia did just that. The young archaeologist tried very hard to push for Arab states that would respect national and tribal loyalties, but at the last minute was overruled by the Sykes-Picot Agreement of 1916. Russia agreed to the power lines drawn, and the rest is history.

OPPOSITE ABOVE
Spies, lies and battle-lines: the biblical Battle of Carchemish was fought by Egypt and Assyria against the forces of Babylon. The former were defeated by the remarkable Nebuchadnezzar II in a epic battle descibed in the Book of Jeremiah.

OPPOSITE BELOW
Gertrude Bell knew how to pack a tent as well as a pistol.

hands of Nebuchadnezzar, King of the Babylonians, in 605 BCE.

It was here that Lawrence learned Arabic, and began a fascination with the Middle East that was to inspire the rest of his life.

During an eventful trip to the Ile de Graye, near Aqaba, Lawrence and Woolley managed to secure the secret blueprints for the railway from a disgruntled Italian engineer. Three years later, Lawrence was commissioned into the British army and, given his specialized knowledge of the region, detailed to the British Military Intelligence Department in Cairo. He was at the head of a camel-mounted Arab army when Aqaba fell in July 1917. The famous victory was memorialized in the 1962 film *Lawrence of Arabia*.

Lawrence wasn't alone. The remarkable, pistol-packing Gertrude Bell was an invaluable resource for British Intelligence's Arab Bureau. She, too, had travelled widely in the desert, wearing a divided skirt that allowed her to ride like a man.

In 1916, Bell spied on Iraqi tribal activities around Basra. Soon, she was enlisted as the first female military intelligence officer, tasked with assessing Arab willingness to join Lawrence's anti-Ottoman revolt.

Bell was more of a cultural *agent provocateur* than an archaeologist *per se*. She helped transform attitudes to the region, and wrote the Antiquities legislation that prevented Europe's museums from simply scooping up the Middle East's entire culture. She later became the honorary Director of Antiquities for Iraq. During her many trips, she also photographed and documented hundreds of ancient and

mediaeval structures, from Assyrian, Babylonian and Hittite archaeological sites to the minarets, mosques and palaces of early Islam.

The spying traffic wasn't all one-way. In Ireland, in the 1930s, the German Director of the National Museum, Adolf Mahr, was arrested and accused of being a Nazi spy helping to plan Hitler's invasion of Ireland.

In 1917, soldiers arrested a pith-helmet-wearing American as he was about to photograph an old Spanish fort along the Honduran coast. Sylvanus Morley complained to the commanding officer: he was a specialist in Mesoamerican archaeology. He had great *chutzpah*: the true purpose of his trip was to hunt for German shortwave broadcast stations and submarine bases in Central America.

Morley was one of many American archaeologists and anthropologists who used their profession as cover for gathering intelligence. This patriotic willingness is perhaps not surprising. Alfred Kidder, a famous figure in American archaeology circles, served as an officer in the infantry in France; Charles Peabody taught military science. During the war, the whole top floor of the Peabody Museum at Harvard was converted to a military radio school, while part of the first floor became classrooms for the Army Training Corps. Almost the entire museum staff was involved in the war effort.

ARCHAEOLOGY DURING WORLD WAR II

The advent of World War II may have put some excavations on hold, as would be the case with the survey of Sutton Hoo in the south of England (see page 165), but one man remained fascinated by the secrets that archaeology could uncover.

In 1938, when Adolf Hitler paid a state visit to Rome, the Italian fascist leader Mussolini, who had once declared how much he hated German tourists brandishing guidebooks, laid on a huge

BELOW
Binbirkilise in Lycaonia, in modern-day Turkey: one of the sites Bell helped to excavate and document. The Byzantine centre's name means "one thousand and one churches".

welcome and an elaborate night-time
motor cavalcade. The commanding
beauty of ancient Rome was illuminated
by 45,000 modern electric lamps, linked
by 100 miles (160 km) of cabling.
The Colosseum, that potent symbol of
imperial power, was lit from inside by
red lamps that cast a bloody glow on the
grass. It fascinated Hitler.

Like many before him, Hitler drew
lessons from Imperial Rome, and one of
those was that Rome had been a cultural
cuckoo. It had greedily assimilated
other influences, worshipped other
nations' gods and, in so doing, turned
its opponents' own soldiers against
themselves. At all costs, Hitler would
prepare Germany for what he saw as
its destiny: creating and controlling the
1,000-year Reich.

In December 1938, a small expedition
struggled slowly northwards into the
Himalayas. The steep and treacherous
mountain paths led them ever higher,
but their 50 mules were holding up and
the Swastika flag still hung stiffly in the
freezing air. The leader was Ernst Schäfer,
like the four other scientists with him
a member of the *Ahnenerbe*, the Nazi
Ancestral Heritage Organization. At the
heart of its research was the investigation
of the origins and spread of the Ayran race.
So what on earth were they doing in Tibet?

They were searching for the
prehistoric origins of humanity. The
theory seems to have sprung from the
German philosopher Immanuel Kant,
who labelled Tibet the birthplace of
creation. He named the first, mighty
race of people "Aryan" – a name derived
from the Sanskrit word *arya*, meaning
"noble". Mystics had later taken things
further, and announced that there had
once been seven "root" races in the
history of humanity. One of them had
first appeared on a long-lost island
in the middle of the Atlantic Ocean:
the legendary island of Atlantis, first
described by the philosopher Plato.
Survivors from Atlantis took refuge in
the natural fastness of the Himalayas
and established a new kingdom called
Shangri-La, a Tibetan Eden. Along the
way, they passed on their great knowledge

and wisdom to the Aryans. This was the world's first "diffusion theory".

The party's 26-year-old anthropologist, Bruno Beger, made detailed records of the bemused locals, taking fingerprints and carefully checking facial characteristics, hair and eye colour. He became convinced that the Aryan master race was weakened after the survivors of Atlantis mixed with Tibetans. Sensing that war would soon break out and prevent them getting home, the team beat a hurried retreat after taking 2,200 photographs.

The *Ahnenerbe* was in the business of myth-making. The hunt for Hitler's cherished Aryans was carefully tailored to prove that the Aryans from whom

the modern German race was meant to have descended had lit the first torch of civilization. The only problem was, where were Germany's magnificent, prehistoric temples? The Nazis would have to find them elsewhere....

An expedition took place to the Swedish island of Bohuslan to document petroglyphs that were, it was argued, evidence of a Bronze Age Aryan language. Himmler's Excavations department, transferred from the SS, financed 18 excavations, including many on Crete, long regarded as the potential home of the first European civilization.

Ernst Schäfer, a zoologist by training, was put in charge of excavations at

Biskupin in Poland, a remarkable settlement whose fortress dates from the Iron Age. The extraordinary thing about Biskupin is that its sophisticated defences are built on an artificial island. This level of early technological innovation convinced the *Ahnenerbe* that the settlement must be "Aryan".

Preserved in marshland at the edge of a huge lake, the fortress was defended by a timber and earth wall 19 ft (6 m) high, and 1,500 ft (450 m) in circumference. It was constructed with parallel walls of logs, linked by cross pieces packed with clay. A belt of fir and oak poles was driven into the lake bottom at a 45-degree angle. It acted as a breakwater,

an ice-breaker in the winter, and of course, provided an excellent first level of defence against attack.

The popular view is that Iron Age Europe was somehow wild and undisciplined, but Biskupin suggests otherwise: it had individual streets, public spaces, storerooms and more than 100 houses, while a wooden causeway, with a watchtower, made a link to the mainland. No wonder the Nazis wanted to lay claim to it. Modern dendrochronology of the oak used dates Biskupin's creation to the winter of 738–737 BCE.

In Germany itself, Assien Bohmers was busily digging up evidence from

ABOVE
An ancestral Aryan race? When the *Ahnenerbe* funded historian Franz Altheim to study rock art in Italy's Camonica valley, he began to see Nazi ideologies written into the stone. Above is a detail from a deer hunt. The huge site's history stretches through the Bronze Age and Iron Age, and the local petroglyph tradition was revived in medieval times.

LEFT
Ancient relief from the necropolis of Naqsh-e Rustam,
near the ruins of Persepolis in Persia, showing the triumph
of Shapur I over the Roman Emperor Valerian and Philip
the Arab.

the Palaeolithic era, when *Homo sapiens* shared the tundra with woolly mammoths and sabre-tooth tigers.

One of the most extraordinary theories came courtesy of Walter Wurst, who believed that the warlike ancient Persians were in fact Aryans, who had supposedly lost their innate superiority due to racial intermixing. Wurst proposed an expedition to Iran to investigate the spectacular site of Naqsh-e Rustam, in the sacred mountains near Persepolis, where an inscription describes the Achaemenid emperor Darius I as an "Aryan".

While Himmler's scientists, explorers and folk historians let ideology overrule their intellectual integrity, German archaeologists were sent further afield to plunder museums and carry out illegal excavations. During the Nazi occupation of Greece, its troops used the gateway to the Acropolis as a latrine. Anti-aircraft batteries were placed inside the Parthenon, which ironically enough was itself a memorial to a devastating war.

THE FORTRESS OF THE LAKE

The lifespan of excavations at Biskupin in Poland neatly encapsulates the huge changes in archaeology that took place after World War II. After being abandoned, the island had gradually been reclaimed by the lake, and the anaerobic marshland had the incredible effect of preserving the wooden city.

Before the discovery of this settlement and its remarkable lake fortress, it was assumed that the prehistoric local Lusatian culture was entirely transient. In almost a century of work, archaeologists at Biskupin have learned vast amounts about this era of prehistory. In the process of tackling

ABOVE
Water played a key role in the preservation of the Iron Age site at Biskupin, in Poland. The buildings seen today are an extensive reconstruction dating from the second half of the 20th century.

this huge challenge, they made many decisions that redefined archaeology for the 20th century.

Work started in 1933. It was a multi-disciplinary team, and unlike many excavations before it, came from the heart of a university. It was led by a Polish archaeologist, Professor Józef Kostrzewski of Poznan University.

Biskupin was a massive archaeological challenge, involving work in treacherous and often cold conditions, in a race against time and decay. The wet environment also meant that methods usually used in dry conditions weren't always appropriate; new field techniques had to be developed – techniques that are now applied to other wetland sites.

At first, no one realized just how quickly exposure to the open air would destroy the ancient water-logged wood. Lots of experimentation followed, including packing the timbers with salts and trying phenolon resins. Large-scale

excavation had to be halted in 1974, and today, the rest of the structure has been packed back into the earth and deluged with water.

As an academic, Professor Kostrzewski was able to co-opt diverse specialists from other areas of science into the work and open the way for archaeology to link with other disciplines, such as sociology and evolutionary ecology. Biskupin's long-lasting programme of interdisciplinary research has involved archaeo-zoologists, hydrologists, botanists, geologists, architects, palynologists, conservation experts and engineers, as well as divers from the Polish navy. This tradition has continued. Most recently, Dr Mieczysław Sinkiewicz made an extensive study into how Iron Age human occupation over generations affected the local environment.

The Biskupin site is also famous for pioneering "experiential archaeology". In sheds on site, experts re-created Iron Age

ABOVE
Water played a key role in the preservation of the Iron Age site at Biskupin, in Poland. The buildings seen today are an extensive reconstruction dating from the second half of the 20th century.

technology to work out how thousands of years ago people fired pottery, baked bread and forged bronze. They also pioneered experimental breeding of Iron Age livestock: Tarpan-like horses, Red Polish cattle, heath sheep and longhorn goats.

Perhaps most importantly, Biskupin has been used to train new generations of archaeologists, *en masse*. Zdzisław Rajewski, who excavated after the war, set up archaeological training camps on site – the first taking place in 1951. Education programmes also raised understanding about prehistory with the general public and, today, Biskupin hosts an archaeology festival every year.

Archaeology is always massively affected by political circumstances, war being the most extreme. When the Nazis were forced to retreat, they breached the protective dykes around the site and flooded the area, hoping to destroy it. Ironically, that act of vandalism unwittingly helped to preserve the ancient timbers.

At Biskupin, here was a chance to make the past live again, and perhaps find a way of learning to live together, despite occupation and disaster. The project's directors went in for extensive reconstruction; controversial in some other countries, but certainly a positive step in helping the general public engage with history.

Biskupin has a deeper significance, however, to anyone aware of its occupied past. It is a reminder of the many insidious ways that archaeology can be made to serve the state. In Russia,

archaeology had been denounced as "bourgeois" because, pre-revolution, it had always been the domain of the Tsar's court. Antiquarianism was also proscribed, as "the fetishism of objects". Biskupin, on the other hand, had no lordly halls or kingly treasure hoards. When Poland was under Soviet occupation, during 1945–89, Biskupin escaped censure because it was felt to embody an egalitarian spirit; it had been a classless home of "the people".

Nazi and Soviet occupation is just an extreme example; in interpreting archaeology, there is always the risk of contemporary cultural bias. The issue of nationalism, probably more than any other, became a concern of archaeologists post-war, prompting much intellectual angst. The archaeological record is meant to be just that: a record. A body of physical evidence about the past. Any relationship between politics and archaeologists is always going to distort the truth – whatever that turns out to be.

ARCHAEOLOGY COMES OUT OF THE CAVE

Like the human story itself, archaeology will never stand still. Over time, this majestic field of study has helped us towards a much clearer understanding of the development of humanity. Taken out of the hands of the gentleman amateur, it is reinventing itself even now.

Technology is the major disruptive force today. Luckily, there is no discipline more open or more suited to the challenge of reinterpreting the evidence. As the fictional Indiana Jones says in the film *Raiders of the Lost Ark*: "Seventy per cent of archaeology is done in the library. We do not follow maps to buried treasure, and 'X' never, ever marks the spot."

Ironically, though, sophisticated digging tools and 3D detection tools are not

BELOW
The skeleton of a woman aged about 35, from the longhouse at Biskupin, now in the site museum.

always a good thing, at least in the wrong hands. In 2015, police in northeastern China caught 175 tomb looters, who had pillaged a Neolithic archaeological site in northeastern Liaoning province. The operation recovered 1,168 cultural relics worth more than 500 million yuan (HK$630 million). In this age of LiDAR sensors and Global Positioning Systems, it is astounding to think that there are still any archaeological sites left that could yield such riches.

Also extraordinary is the fact that the tomb of Qin Shi Huang, China's very first emperor, remains unexcavated, although the tombs of his "warriors" have been (see pages 70–3). Already, nonetheless, this multinational excavation exemplifies the technical accomplishments of professional archaeologists today. It's a world away from the unbridled, if romantic, chaos of the early 18th- and 19th-century adventurers in Egypt.

LEFT
A major site from the Iron Age: the Nazis also tried to appropriate the archaeology of Biskupin, in Poland.

THE IMMORTAL ARMY

In 1974, a group of Chinese fruit farmers made one of the world's most unexpected discoveries. The area around Mount Li, near the city of Xi'an in Shanxi province, was suffering from a severe drought. Desperate for water for their produce, Yang Quanyi and his five friends decided to dig a well under their persimmon orchard. Quanyi recalled: "Suddenly, I hit the stone man's neck. I told my friend: 'This is a hidden temple.'" He was almost right.

BELOW
The scale of the "Terracotta Army", as it is popularly known, is almost impossible to convey. Rows of lifelike statues extend as far as the eye can see, yet only a small proportion have as yet been excavated.

OPPOSITE
Ruthless and supreme: Emperor Qin Shi Huang.

Inside was a dazzling spectacle: a life-size army of painted clay soldiers that had lain underground for 2,200 years. The massed ranks of terracotta warriors constitute one of the most astonishing finds in the history of archaeology, but form only a tiny part of a long-buried mausoleum built for China's very first emperor, Qin Shi Huang.

There was no record of this burial in existence: no paintings, no stories, not even any local myths. The farmers were astonished. Yet the complex built by the conqueror and war leader who gave his name to the country we know today (Qin is pronounced "Chin") covers an area of 35 sq miles (90.6 sq km).

When Qin came to the throne as a boy in 246 BCE, he ruled a small and not especially powerful state surrounded by many hostile rivals. By 221 BCE, he had conquered not just its closest and most persistent enemy, Chu, but all of the land that we now know as China.

The Qin emperor's grandiose ambitions extended beyond the mortal realm. Believing he could cheat death, he created a subterranean pleasure and fortress complex. It was laid out in beautiful grounds, perhaps an idealized and enhanced version of the extraordinary world he had enjoyed as sovereign. Among the numerous highlights of his vision for the afterlife are twin half-sized chariots embellished with gold and silver – each pulled by a team of four magnificent terracotta horses – and performing troupes of musicians and acrobats.

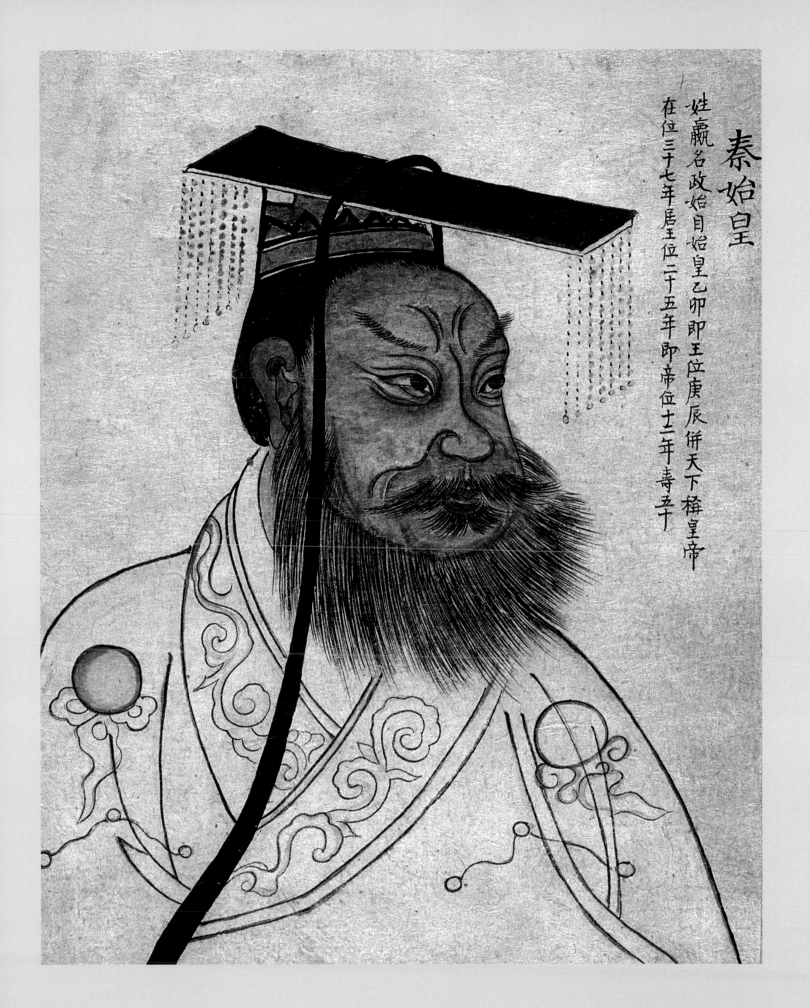

秦始皇

姓嬴名政始自始皇乙卯即王位庚辰併天下稱皇帝
在位三十七年居王位二十五年即帝位十二年壽五十

THE PITS

The clay figures so far discovered lie buried in three pits, just under 1 mile (1.5 km) to the east of the tomb. Some may even be genuine likenesses of the real soldiers who had helped him conquer so much in the span of his 37-year reign. The figure-makers clearly strived for realism. The detail recorded on the thousands of figures, vehicles, animals and equipment in the pits is astonishing – and gives us an unparalleled insight into a vanished empire.

To date, more than 1,100 figures have been restored and now stand vigil in Pit One – but surveys show that more than 6,000 warriors are buried here, with a further 2,000 in Pits Two and Three. Armed with specially produced spears, halberds and swords, even today they are a fearsome and awe-inspiring sight. The power and accuracy of their crossbows in particular would not be matched in Europe for another 2,000 years. Shen

Maosheng, head of the archaeological team, plans to make precise models to help work out their shooting range more accurately.

Researchers are using a novel technique to establish both how the weapons were produced, and how effective they were. The substrate used to make dental moulds is being applied to the metal surfaces, and the resulting highly detailed impressions are examined under a scanning electron microscope. In this way, no harm is done to the actual objects.

The warriors were ranged in Qin battle formation, with the archers in the vanguard and on the flanks protecting a core of heavy infantry and chariots. The researchers are using a pioneering technique, X-ray fluorescence (XRF) spectrometry, to find out what the crossbow bolts were made from. XRF can typically analyse elements from sodium to uranium, and is revolutionizing the way in which archaeologists do their work.

Along with the armies of warriors, the pits contain terracotta models of scribes and scholars, acrobats, musicians and weightlifters. Digs at what were plainly intended to represent outlying gardens have turned up dozens of sculpted waterfowl and birds. Everywhere, there are the stocky brown horses that must have played a key role in Qin-era life.

Most of the huge area is still unexcavated, and archaeologists are keenly aware that subsequent discoveries may change both their view of what they have already found and their view of Qin civilization as a whole.

LEFT
Each warrior is minutely different, a comparative digital study recently found – even the ears.

BELOW
In the on-site workshop, local people have become expert at one of the most daunting jigsaw puzzles in the world: piecing together the warriors, ceramic shard by shard.

ARCHAEOLOGY TODAY

ARCHAEOLOGY TODAY

Nowadays, archaeology is a complex business, involving teams consisting of experts in a diverse range of subjects. But all archaeologists have to begin at the same point: they need to find a place to investigate.

PREVIOUS PAGES
The ruins of Roman baths discovered in Beirut, Lebanon.

LEFT
Tell Brak in Syria, excavated by the British archaeologist Max Mallowan.

BELOW
The Huxley Hoard was discovered using metal detectors.

1. X-RAY FLUORESCENT SPECTROMETRY (XFS): A pioneering technique originally developed for the engineering industry, the latest hand-held device provides a detailed chemical analysis of most materials, including metals, glass and ceramics.

2. GROUND-PENETRATING RADAR (GPR): GPR works by transmitting tiny pulses of energy into a material and recording the strength and the time required for the return of any reflected signal. A series of pulses over a single area make up a scan.

FINDING A SITE

When the crime writer Agatha Christie married archaeologist Max Mallowan in the 1930s, she described walking across hundreds of "tells" in Syria, to try to find the best mound to excavate. They walked so much that her shoes wore out.

Today, archaeologists can employ a variety of technologies to help them pinpoint a likely site for a dig. These can involve everything from metal detectors to satellite imagery.

TECHNOLOGICAL DEVELOPMENTS

Technology is fast transforming archaeology. The discipline is now situated somewhere between the hard, natural sciences, historical studies and the social sciences. Archaeologists are still highly fond of the trowel, but they are also embracing new digital technologies that include:

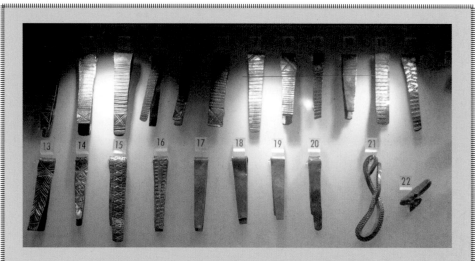

DISCOVERING AN ARCHAEOLOGICAL SITE

There are various ways that a potential site for excavation can be discovered. They include:

- Farmers often make discoveries when ploughing fields
- Construction crews laying foundations or creating tunnels
- Old documents or histories suggesting previous human occupation
- Aerial or satellite surveys
- Local knowledge

ABOVE
Ground-penetrating radar is one of many new technologies archaeologists use to help them discover new sites.

BELOW
The image of a CT scan of an ancient Egyptian mummy is projected above a sarcophagus at an exhibition in Sydney in 2016.

3. ELECTROMAGENTIC INDUCTION (EM):

In its simplest form, EM measures the change in impedance between a transmitter coil and a receiver coil when the magnetic field they generate encounters a conductive material – e.g. a copper object – in the ground. The receiver senses the type and distribution of the material, and identifies it by measuring the induced secondary magnetic field.

4. MOLECULAR FREQUENCY DISCRIMINATOR (MFD):

All elements have a unique "molecular resonant frequency". Gold, for example, resonates at 5 KHz, and silver at 8.7 KHz. The MFD's small transmitter unit generates the frequency that matches the frequency of the target substance.

5. SOFTWARE AND PHOTOGRAPHY:

Chinese researchers working with University College London have found a cheap way to create 3D images of objects – in this case, of the heads of famous Chinese warriors in the Terracotta Army – by taking multiple photographs of each one, and using a "sparse point cloud" software process to map individual details.

6. REMOTE SENSING FROM SPACE:

Near-infrared satellite imagery sweeps the Earth's surface from space, reflecting parts of the electromagnetic spectrum that are invisible to the human eye. The otherwise undetectable changes

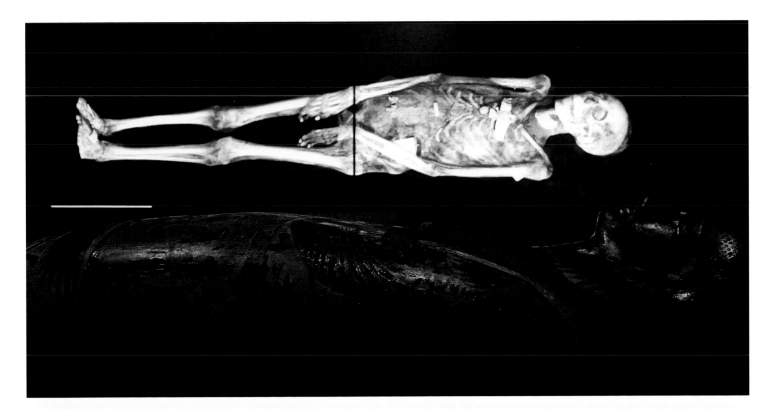

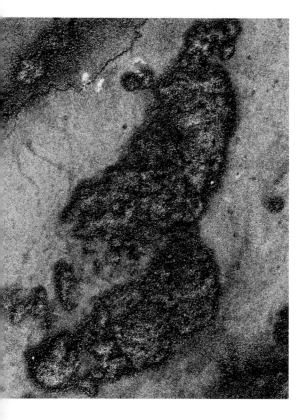

ABOVE
NASA used near-infrared satellite imaging to locate new Mayan archaeological sites.

BELOW
Along the Mississippi, LiDAR has been used to reveal the secrets behind the Effigy Mounds that dot the landscape.

in surface density are then colour-coded by special software. The technology reveals long-hidden patterns and shapes in the landscape and can direct archaeologists to promising excavation sites.

7. AIRBORNE LIDAR (LIGHT DETECTION AND RANGING):
LiDAR employs an airborne laser to measure the exact distance between the scanning equipment and the ground. Multiple laser pulses produce high-definition digital elevation models (DEMs) of the landscape below, which can then be modified and viewed from any angle. It is able to detect height differences of no more than a few centimetres in ground level variations, revealing sites that have lain undetected for centuries.

8. ACCELERATOR MASS SPECTROMETRY (AMS):
AMS radiocarbon dating allows archaeologists to obtain dates from samples that are very much smaller than those needed for standard radiocarbon dating. The accelerator-based mass spectrometer counts *all* of the C14 atoms, rather than just those atoms that are decaying as happens in the standard process, making AMS dates more precise, although it is currently a very expensive process.

AMS is also used to count isotopes. In the late 1980s, archaeologist Douglas Price and geochemist Jim Burton developed a new technique that measured the ratio of strontium isotopes in human bones. It acts as a chemical signature of the local geology within the body.

9. DUAL ENERGY (COMPUTED TOMOGRAPHY) CT SCAN/X-RAY VISUALIZATION:
A CT scanner is a special X-ray machine that takes a series of detailed images of a body. Among other things, the dual CT process can help experts determine what people ate, and what types of disease, if any, they suffered.

DIGGING THE DIRT

Archaeological sites can be difficult to read, unless they are approached with a combination of two things: knowledge and imagination. What looks to the untrained eye like a pile of stones could actually be the entire water system of a Roman building. Once you've found something, how do you date it?

We tend not to give soil a second's thought, but along with water and oxygen, it is what sets Earth apart from other planets. Dirt didn't make its first appearance until 450 million years ago – even though the Earth itself is 4.54 billion years old.

Intimate contact with dirt goes hand in hand with archaeology. To those in the know, soil is like a visible map of time. Lasagne-like, it exists in layers, one built on top of another. There are two aspects to this: the first is stratification, and the second is the geological law of superposition. Steno's law holds that the oldest layers of earth are those that are closest to the centre of the earth.

STRATIFICATION: Natural processes cause the layering of soils – a river eroding its banks and then depositing a layer of silt, for instance. But even without the action of rivers, it is surprising how much matter can build up at an abandoned place. Structures decay, crumble and gradually return to the land. Water, wind and gravity carry soil from high or exposed regions to deposit it in more sheltered areas. This mixes with leaf and plant mould, and the whole process starts over again.

Sometimes, geological strata can be confusing. Erosion, rodent burrows, or posts driven into the soil can make the stratigraphy much more difficult to read because they disturb the original, natural layers. For archaeologists, however, these intrusions are important, as they are often the product of human behaviour.

Stratigraphy creates a context, a framework of time and space that is everything to an archaeologist. Once a shard of pottery or a fragment of

LEFT
An example of archaeological
stratigraphy from Goosehill Camp
in Sussex.

BELOW & BOTTOM English
archaeologist Edward Harris, seen
here (on the left) in the field in the
1970s, invented the Harris Matrix,
a way of "mapping" the stratigraphic
sequence. Each of the four sections of
the excavation are recorded and drawn
up, and combined into a single sequence
in the centre of the diagram, which
represents the evolution of the site
through relative time.

jewellery is out of the ground, its
context is lost. The archaeologist's
goal is to detect and record the web of
information between an object and its
context that allows them to reconstruct
a chain of events. In other words, not
just what happened, but how and why it
happened.

Over the 250 years that archaeologists
have been recording and dating, they
have created intricate "typologies" for
objects such as pottery and stone tools
that change in style over the centuries and
help date specific layers. This is known as
"relative" dating.

So how to record all this information?
There is a universal system for
documenting site stratigraphy with a
visual cross-section, called the Harris
Matrix. Dr Edward Harris came up
with it in the 1970s when working on
a large-scale, urban site in the English
town of Winchester. He wanted to record
the material clearly, in ways that future
excavators could understand. These days
the original layers and positions of finds
and samples are also measured, digitized
and registered in GIS-programmes, and
can even be rendered in 3D, but they are
still using this basic conceptual technique.

THE HUMAN FACTOR: There are
both "naturally" and "culturally" created
soil layers, and as you'd expect, towns and
cities have their own complications, called
human beings. They themselves add to
the accumulating layers, and the picture
can be quite confusing.

To make the archaeological picture
more complicated, people also burn,
abandon or tear down the buildings their
ancestors built. They then build on top of
the ruins, making urban sites much more
complex than rural ones.

Garbage, or anything that people no
longer have a use for, eventually, through the

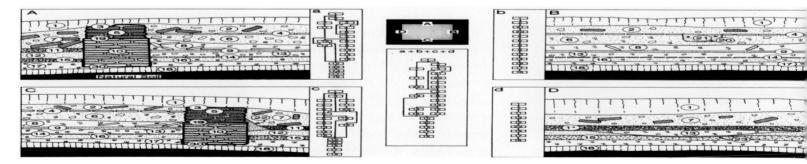

DISEASE: Ancient afflictions, trauma or congenital disease do show up in bones. Various types of records including historical documents, medical instruments and of course art can tell us about the illnesses people have suffered from. Not many infections reach the bone. Acute diseases such as the plague and smallpox tend to kill or be cured very quickly and do not have time to affect the skeleton, nor do diseases such as measles, smallpox, plague and flu, although tuberculosis does.

Congenital diseases are the most common diseases found in skeletal material. They include osteoarthritis, osteoporosis, and general changes associated with the ageing process.

NUTRITION: Radiography, CT scanning, microscopic analysis and DNA analysis can all reveal information about diet and health. Iron deficiency anaemia, vitamin D deficiency and the haemorrhaging that comes with scurvy all show up on bones.

TEETH: Through teeth, archaeology gives us a long-term view of human health. There was a time when museum curators carefully cleaned up their exhibits. Not any more: thanks to the dental calculus, or mineralized dental plaque on their teeth, we now realize that Neanderthals weren't entirely carnivorous, as once assumed. They ate a mixed diet and even turned to plants for pain relief.

CIRCULATORY PROBLEMS: If the blood supply to an area of bone is cut off, that area of the skeleton will die and may be reabsorbed. *Osteochondritis dissecans* is a relatively common disease which falls into this category and tends to be associated with physical trauma.

CARBON DATING

Carbon is everywhere: in the atmosphere, in the earth and in the oceans. The invention of radiocarbon dating has changed the way we see the oceans, rocks and soils of earth. It has also given us completely new insights about human history.

There are two main methods of dating archaeological finds. "Relative" dating means working by association: studying the types of tools or pottery finds and comparing them with others from the same culture. This is called seriation. The other method is called "Absolute" dating. This is a misnomer, as even high-technology techniques are not exactly "absolute", making more of a reasonable approximation.

There are a number of "Absolute" techniques, but it was radiocarbon dating that caused the revolution. The process can determine the age of anything from an Egyptian mummy to a prehistoric poppy. Its inventor, American chemist Willard Libby, won a Nobel prize for his invention, just in time to help authenticate some of the most controversial documents in the world: the Dead Sea scrolls (see page 233).

CARBON-14/RADIOCARBON:

Carbon-14 is the ticking clock inside each and every one of us. Also known as radiocarbon, it is generated in the upper atmosphere and enters our bodies through natural processes like breathing, or eating the plants that themselves take in carbon to grow.

There are three types of carbon isotope: Carbon-12, Carbon-13 and Carbon-14. Unlike 12 and 13, the radioactive isotope Carbon-14 is highly unstable. When a creature dies, the radiocarbon begins to decay. The rate of its decay can be measured and compared with the levels of other carbon atoms. That ratio establishes a chronology for any once-living organism. Its usual range is up to 30,000 years, but with sensitive (and expensive) instruments, it's possible to push this further, possibly even up to 70,000 years.

Libby initially calibrated his "clock" by dating objects of known age such as Egyptian mummies and bread from Pompeii. Today, it is measured against the known ages of tree rings. As a rule, carbon dates are younger than calendar dates:

20,000 carbon years roughly equates to 24,000 calendar years.

The new dating technique has changed our approach to archaeology itself. The very fact it exists has made it possible to take a broader look at human prehistory. Combined with the astonishing advances in DNA science, we are now able to begin rewriting the entire map of human life on Earth.

DIFFICULTIES WITH DATING:

The amount of carbon-14 in the atmosphere fluctuates, affected by cosmic radiation and factors on earth such as volcanoes or sudden upsurges in pollution, both of which belch carbon into the air. Nuclear tests in the 1950s and 1960s had a big impact on carbon-14 levels in the world's atmosphere. In the early days of radiocarbon dating, this was a problem. A huge amount of work has gone on since then to create an internationally-agreed, historical "calibration" curve that takes changing carbon levels into account.

BELOW
Tree rings are used to calibrate carbon dating techniques.

THE ORIGINS OF HUMANKIND

THE ORIGINS OF HUMANKIND

In the 1800s, most people believed the Earth was about 6,000 years old, because of the accounts written in the Bible about the Creation. Archaeology was about to unravel these assumptions. In 1856, in the serene Neander Valley in Germany, workers quarrying for limestone dug out heavy bones like those of a bear and a strange, human-like skull. A local schoolteacher, Johann Carl Fuhlrott, had to save them from the spoil heap. The skull had a prominent brow and deep eye sockets.

A keen amateur naturalist, Fuhlrott turned to the Professor of Anatomy at the University of Bonn, Hermann Schaaffhausen. He was convinced that they belonged to a "savage and barbarous" race of humans. It soon emerged that other bones like these were being found across Europe.

The discovery of Neanderthals, a human-like species that was nevertheless not human, became a key piece of evidence supporting the direct evolutionary link between modern humans and apes. *Homo sapiens* was not unique after all, but merely one of several types of early human species. Over

ABOVE TOP RIGHT
Johann Carl Fuhlrott, who set in motion the identification of Neanderthals.

ABOVE
A skull of *Homo neanderthalensis*, 30,000–50,000 years old.

THE ANCESTORS OF HUMANITY

*c.*4.5 million years ago–2 million years ago *Australopithecus*	2.4 million years ago–1.4 million years ago *Homo habilis*	1.9 million years ago–143,000 years ago *Homo erectus*	600,000–200,000 years ago *Homo heidelbergensis*	400,000 years ago–*c.*40,000 years ago *Homo neanderthalis*	*c.*200,000 years ago–present *Homo sapiens*

the following years, further evidence of human ancestors continued to emerge.

LUCY AND NAIA

In 1974, the American anthropologist Donald Johanson discovered the skeleton of "Lucy" in Ethiopia, an *Australopithecus afarensis*, a precursor species to humanity that had lived 3.2 million years ago.

Once modern humans evolved, they gradually spread across the globe. From their origins in Africa, they first moved into southern Asia and Europe, and from there expanded into Australasia, Polynesia and the Americas. There were two waves of migration, the first through North Africa 130,000–115,000 years ago and the second following the southern coast of Asia 77,000–69,000 years ago.

"Naia", named after the water nymphs of mythology, is one of the oldest and most complete human skeletons discovered in the Americas. The body was found wholly by chance, in waters 140 ft (42.6 m) below water in a spectacular cave in Mexico's Yucatán Peninsula. On an expedition funded by *National Geographic*, Mexican divers Alberto Nava Alejandro Alvarez and Franco Attolini explored an immense underwater crevasse they called Hoyo Negro, the "black hole". There, they saw the remains of a teenage girl who had

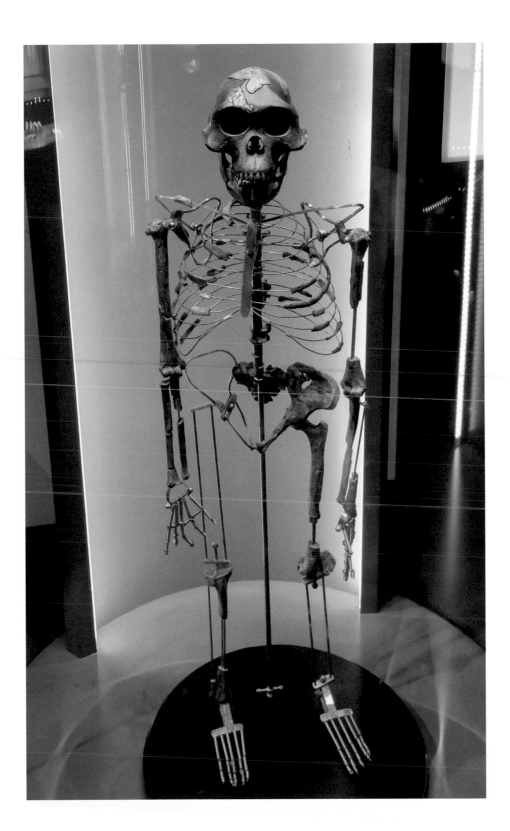

RIGHT
The skeleton of Lucy (*Australopithecus afarensis*), displayed in the Natural History Museum of Vienna.

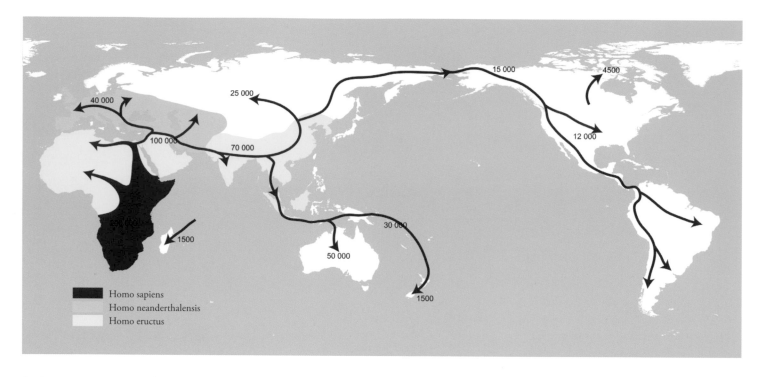

40 000

100 000

200 000

1500

25 000

70 000

50 000

30 000

1500

15 000

12 000

4500

■ Homo sapiens
Homo neanderthalensis
Homo eructus

died 13,000 years ago; the young woman was lying on a small ledge.

Naia's skeleton was left surprisingly intact. Amazingly, it was still possible to extract DNA from her teeth, and for experts studying her skull to reconstruct her facial features. When her DNA was studied by Mexico's National Institute of Anthropology and History, it shed fresh light on a big controversy: who were the first Americans, and how did they arrive in the Western Hemisphere? Her DNA, with clear links to modern Native Americans,

strengthened the evidence for the Bering Land Bridge theory (see pages 170).

STONE AGE CULTURES

In the 18th century scholars began to notice evidence of human activity – stone tools like axes, hammers, flints and arrowheads – buried deep in the ground. The realization was a key moment in the development of stratigraphy.

In East Africa, palaeontologists have

ABOVE
The spread of *Homo sapiens* from Africa around the world, over thousands, and even tens and hundreds of thousands, of years (see also page 87).

BELOW LEFT
A diver carefully brushes debris from the skull of Naia.

BELOW RIGHT
A hand-axe from Olduvai Gorge, over a million years old, now in the British Museum.

JOHN FRERE'S "WEAPONS OF WAR"

In 1797, the English antiquary John Frere found ancient artefacts deep in the ground while digging in a clay pit in Suffolk. He was sure they were weapons, but they were under sand and embedded underneath 12 ft (4 m) of undisturbed soil. The sand layer also held shells and the remains of tiny marine creatures. How could any "weapons of war", which must have been made by man, have at one stage been beneath the sea? John Frere's "weapons of war" were later recognized as Acheulean hand-axes, so named after the archaeological site in France where the tools were first identified, St Acheul.

LEFT
Hand-axes from Hoxne in Suffolk, unearthed by Frere.

BELOW LEFT
Louis and Mary Leakey, absorbed in studying fossilized fragments of skull.

found many sophisticated tools that pre-date the emergence of *Homo sapiens*. Other hominids could make tools. In 1929, the Kenyan Louis Leakey visited Olduvai Gorge in Tanzania in search of fossils, but found some of the earliest hand-made tools ever discovered. The site held more than 2,000 stone tools including hand-axes, scrapers and stitching awls. With his wife, Mary, he began studying an unimaginably ancient time.

The finds dated back to approximately 1.8 million years ago – before modern humans had even evolved. Further research by Sonia Harmand and Jason Lewis in 2011 uncovered even older tools. They found 20 artefacts at the Lomekwi site in Kenya dating back 3.3 million years: the first known material evidence of human history.

In the Upper Palaeolithic, approximately 40,000 years ago, a

STONE AGE ERAS

Paleolithic
2.6 million years
ago–10,000 years ago

Mesolithic
20,000–9500 BCE – The Levant
9660–500 BCE – Europe

Neolithic
10,000–4,500 BCE

THE LASCAUX CAVES

In the village of Montignac in southwestern France, a local teenage boy, Marcel Ravidat, and three of his friends, armed with only a lamp to guide their way, ventured into a deep cave searching for treasure. They found a treasure of an entirely different sort – the walls were covered with prehistoric paintings. These depict animal and human figures, using ochre and other mineral pigments. In 1950, the paintings at Lascaux were Carbon-14 dated at 17,000 years old. It is not just the paintings that fascinate experts: there are almost 1,500 engravings, several signs and holes in the wall that indicate prehistoric scaffolding used to create the paintings. Visitor numbers over the years threatened Lascaux and, as a result, even older cave art (discovered by potholers in 1994) at Chauvet Cave, in the Ardèche Gorge in southern France, can be viewed only in replica form, at a major new visitor centre which documents a full 50,000 years of dramatic cave art in the region.

THE "RED LADY OF PAVILAND"

The Paviland Cave in South Wales is a lonely place, accessible only at low tide and requiring a sheer climb to reach it. Thirty-five thousand years ago, a group of hunter-gatherers hauled a body up the steep slope to this magnificent position. At that time, sea levels were much lower and the cave looked out over a 70-mile (115-km)-wide plain teeming with wildlife. As they laid him to rest, the group smeared the body with red ochre, decorated it with painted shells and surrounded it with ivory – showing extraordinary commitment to someone who must have been very important. The remains were first discovered and named in 1823 by the Reverend William Buckland, an eccentric Professor of Geology at Oxford University, who decided that the skeleton must be a woman – a witch or prostitute from the Roman era. As we now know, it was in fact the body of a man and the site is one of the oldest ceremonial burials ever found in Europe.

revolution took place. The crude tools of the past were replaced with far more complex technologies, social structures and cultural practices. Bows and spears were invented to make hunting easier. Art, ritual and religion began to emerge. Artwork has been found at caves at Lascaux, Cosquer Cave and Chauvet Cave in France, ranging in age from 30,000 to 17,000 years ago.

It was not only in Africa that prehistoric bones upset ideas on human development. The "Red Lady of Paviland" may have revealed intricate burial practices on the part of our early hunter-gatherer forebears, but a vast pit at Sima de los Huesas in Spain showed that some hominids buried their dead in mass graves. These earliest-known residents of Europe lived between 1.2 million and 600,000 years ago.

ABOVE TOP
Paviland Cave (also known as Goat's Hole Cave), on the Gower Peninsula in South Wales, where the ochre-coloured skeleton was discovered.

ABOVE
Victorian academic William Buckland.

OPPOSITE
Depiction of a megaloceros, from the Lascaux Caves, a rich source of information about prehistoric life.

CRADLES OF CIVILIZATION

THE FERTILE CRESCENT

About 9 miles (15 km) from the city of Sanliurfa in Turkey is the oldest sacred temple ever discovered in the world: Göbekli Tepe. It dates back 12,000 years. The extraordinary finds at this site have forced us to rewrite the story of human history. A civilization capable of advanced architecture and symbolic art is not supposed to have existed so long ago.

From 3500 BCE onwards, a series of developed city-states began to appear in Sumer, the fertile area of Mesopotamia between the Tigris and the Euphrates rivers. This is the first place that writing was invented, in pictographs and then cuneiform script, and also where the first world's earliest cities developed.

Historians have often called the Middle East "the cradle of civilization".

In particular, they refer to the Fertile Crescent – a wide sweep of land that reaches from the Persian Gulf to present-day Lebanon, Israel, Jordan and Egypt. Conventional wisdom holds that civilization could only begin once people had stopped being nomadic, settled down and begun to live in farming communities. Only then, the argument goes, did people have the time and

resources to create complex social systems and religious structures. It is now believed that this "revolution" was carried out by many hands, at many places, over thousands of years.

At the far northern edge of the Fertile Crescent sits Göbekli Tepe, meaning "Potbelly Hill" in Turkish. Its excavation has been a revelation. It suggests that the first sparks of civilization were driven by the

c.10,000 BCE	c.5500 BCE	2500 BCE–	c. 2334 BCE–	1894 BCE	c.1600 BCE –
The earliest Neolithic places of worship are established at Göbekli Tepe	Sumer is settled in Mesopotamia	605BCE Assyrian Empire	2154 BCE Akkadian Empire	First Babylonian Dynasty emerges, centring around Babylon	c.1180 BCE Hittite Empire

ABOVE
Cryptic puzzle: Cuneiform writing.

LEFT
Klaus Schmidt, whose intuition led him to the Göbekli Tepe site.

need to worship. When the site was first discovered in the 1960s, it was dismissed as an abandoned medieval cemetery. The German archaeologist Klaus Schmidt decided to investigate the site again in 1994. So far only 1 acre (0.4 hectare) of a potential 22-acre (9-hectare) site has been excavated. Schmidt and his team mapped the entire summit using ground penetrating radar and geomagnetic surveys, with the result that the site is thought to hold 16 other megalithic rings.

| **_c._1200 BCE–546 BCE**
Lydian Empire | **911 BCE–609 BCE**
Neo-Assyrian Empire | **626 BCE–539 BCE**
Neo-Babylonian or Chaldean Empire | **678 BCE–549 BCE**
Median Empire | **_c._550 BCE–330 BCE**
Achaemenid Empire | **330 BCE**
Alexander the Great takes control of the Persian Empire |

READING THE HEAVENS

Klaus Schmidt and his team uncovered a series of mystical temples, in circles of beautifully carved pillars of stone. The temples' strange pillars are T-shaped, and the largest are 18 ft (5.5 m) high, weighing 17.5 tons (16 tonnes). Some are blank, but others are elaborately carved with imagery: writhing snakes, spiders, gazelles and bulls. Schmidt thought it possible that the pillars are stylized representations of human beings. Even more astonishing is that 6,000 years before the invention of writing, and seven millennia before the Great Pyramid of Giza was built, the central temple on the hill appears – to some – to map out the zodiac. It had long been thought that the first astronomers were the ancient Babylonians. Central to the temple known to the excavators as Temple D is a sequence of 12 pillars – the magical 12 that marks our calendar months today, the same 12 we use on our clocks. What is thought to be the world's oldest calendar (in monument form) was found in Scotland in 2004: it, too, works on a sequence of 12. The Warren Field site, however, dates from three and a half millennia later than Göbekli Tepe. Scientists from the University of Edinburgh believe that the first temple at Göbekli Tepe was a religious observatory, marking the history of comets and meteor showers. The bird and scorpion symbolism on one particular pillar, named the Vulture Stone, appears to document a comet strike around 11,000 BCE. If it happened at all, this devastating event would have caused environmental chaos and a mini ice age: whether or not it did occur is highly controversial among scientists. Carbon dating of charcoal deposits provides a date for the Vulture Stone that appears to mesh with new geological evidence from the Greenland ice core.

ABOVE
Lamassu: an Assyrian protective deity.

LEFT
The enigmatic Vulture stone.

Göbekli Tepe is only one of the Fertile Crescent's many archaeological sites, testament to an extraordinarily rich and vivid human past. The sad truth is that in a politically volatile region, modern war is reshaping the archaeological landscape in new and unwelcome ways. Many historic cities, such as Nimrud and Nineveh, are now at risk of destruction. Much of the damage is premeditated and deliberate: the forces of so-called Islamic State actively seek to obliterate humanity's cultural treasures. Zealots used power tools to destroy the colossal lamassu,

statdues of terrifying human-headed winged beasts that stood guard at the Nergal Gate in Nineveh, and in Aleppo, Syria's oldest city, more than a hundred historic buildings have been damaged beyond repair.

CITIES OF BEAUTY

From the Middle Ages, what most Europeans knew about ancient Mespotamia was what they read in the Bible – stories of the Creation, the Flood and Babylon's Tower of Babel.

The gifted linguist Claudius James Rich became the Resident in Baghdad in 1808. Rich was the first antiquarian to examine the ancient site of Babylon, beginning in 1811–12. It was the starting point of Mesopotamian archaeology.

ABOVE
The British Resident of Baghdad, James Claudius Rich.

RIGHT
A stone relief depicting the Assyrian king, Sargon II, with one of his dignitaries.

UR – CITY OF THE MOON GOD

The city of Ur, named after the Moon god Urin, was occupied as early as the 7th millennium BCE. Early investigations in the 1920s led archaeologists to believe that they had found the site of the Biblical flood. However, the evidence of erosion was in fact due to regular smaller-scale flooding from the Euphrates and Tigris rivers.

One of the earliest western visitors to Ur with archaeological ambitions was the Italian musician and author Pietro della Valle in 1625, who returned home with a number of inscribed bricks. The first significant excavation of the site was conducted by the British Vice Consul at Basra, John George Taylor, in 1853–54, working on behalf of the British Museum. Taylor found a cylinder bearing the name of Nabonidus (see pages 20–1) in the ziggurat that is now one of the major features of the site.

RIGHT
Leonard Woolley at work, excavating the ruins of Ur.

BELOW
The "war panel" on the Royal Standard of Ur.

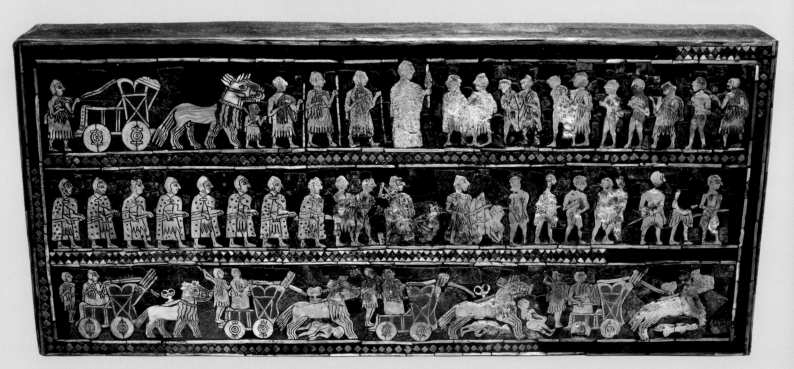

In 1923, during an expedition to Ur led by Leonard Woolley, excavations uncovered a royal cemetery whose oldest tombs dated as far back as 2600 BCE. From the tomb of Queen Puabi, who lived *c.*2500 BCE, emerged beautiful artefacts including a wooden harp, inlaid with exquisite ornamentation, and a bull's head, with staring lapis lazuli eyes. Nine superb headdresses were found, made from lapis and carnelian, their fringes of beech and willow leaves beaten from pure gold. This quality of workmanship is evidence of a stable, prosperous and technologically advanced society. Yet the headdresses lent a macabre glory to the skulls of the dead women wearing them.

Every single one of the 16 royal tombs was a place of ritual sacrifice. As many as 80 people at a time – courtiers, servants, soldiers and musicians – were sacrificed. Dressed in their most gorgeous finery, each held a cup of poison. Once the last had swallowed the lethal mix, the living lit ritual fires and celebrated the dead with a funeral banquet. We don't know if they volunteered or were forced.

In another tomb, Woolley discovered what is known as the Royal Standard of Ur, since he believed it would have been carried on a pole. The "war panel" shows the city's army marching to defeat a naked and quailing enemy. It is the earliest representation of a Sumerian military force.

Woolley's dig lasted until 1934. The objects uncovered were divided between the British Museum and the University of Pennsylvania Museum of Archaeology and Anthropology. The Iraqi authorities hope to develop the site as a tourist destination and, in 2009, agreed to work with the University of Pennsylvania on further excavations there.

Lebanon, Israel, Gaza and Syria between 1500 BCE and 539 BCE. They grew rich trading slaves, precious metals, wine, dye and pottery. They were so influential that their alphabet and language spread throughout the Mediterranean.

In 1923 the French archaeologist Pierre Montet discovered inscriptions made in the Phoenician alphabet on the sarcophagus of Ahiram, a king from the city of Byblos. There, Montet uncovered nine royal tombs in the city that gave its name both to books and to the Bible. In recent years, an excavation in the city of Sidon has revealed a fascinating collection of artefacts.

Despite their influence in the ancient world, most of the archaeological evidence for the great civilization comes from their neighbours. Reliefs found at the Assyrian city of Nineveh show Phoenician warships in great detail, including the dramatic eyes painted on their prows.

Phoenician explorers ventured as far afield as the Atlantic Ocean and established trading parternships with the British Isles and Scandinavia. They established colonies such as Carthage in North Africa, which they used to spread their culture, including the worship of Ba'al and other gods, around the Mediterranean.

RIGHT
In the southern Lebanese city of Sidon, a dig revealed a large quantity of Phoenician pottery.

THE LAND OF THE PHARAOHS

Ever since the discoveries of Napoléon's expedition, no other civilization has held such allure and excitement in the popular imagination as ancient Egypt. Archaeologists, historians and travellers have flocked to the country to see its marvels for themselves.

LEFT
Jean-François Champollion, who made the key breakthrough in deciphering Egyptian hieroglyphs.

FAR LEFT
Champollion's notes on Egyptian grammar.

BELOW
The Rosetta Stone with its inscriptions in three languages.

The Egyptians had left so much to document their lives and tell their stories, but how to decipher their inscriptions, paintings and papyri?

In 1820, Jean-François Champollion began his race with the British polymath Thomas Young to decipher hieroglyphics. The key was a mysterious black stone, dug up by Napoléon's soldiers, and inscribed with three versions of a decree. Young had worked out the specific letters in Ptolemy V's name, found on the Rosetta stone and the Philae obelisk. Champollion was the first to realize that the language was based on both pictures – ideographs – and phonetic sounds.

One beneficiary was Auguste Mariette. The Louvre Museum, keen to keep its lead in Egyptology, sent the young amateur devotee of hieroglyphics to buy new collections of papyri. Failing in this, he turned to a local Bedouin tribe, who took him to Saqqara. There, among a "spectacle of desolation" he found a huge temple complex, approached by a ceremonial avenue of sphinxes. When he returned to France, it was with a cache of some 2,500 statues, bronzes and cartouches. With the help of Isma'il Pasha, he made history in 1853 by opening a museum in Cairo. In 1858, he was appointed as Director of the Department of Antiquities.

To Mariette's practical work on the ground would soon be added major advancements in techniques and scholarship with figures like William Flinders Petrie. Significant milestones in the history of archaeology, but Egyptology had further gifts to reveal.

One hundred years after Champollion had shown how to crack the code of hieroglyphs, another archaeologist, Howard Carter, took centre stage with a team of expert restorers, language experts, chemists and natural scientists. After various unsuccessful attempts, in November 1922, Carter was almost certain that he had found the tomb of the long lost "Boy King" Tutankhamun, in Luxor's Valley of the Kings (see pages 108–9).

The event generated more publicity than any other "moment" in the history of the science. Yet how much more extraordinary is it that the tomb of Ramesses II, "The Great", who died at the age of around 90, was just a few feet away?

BELOW
Mariette discovered these sphinxes, now held at the Louvre, which originally marked a ceremonial temple pathway.

THE GREATEST FIND IN HISTORY

"Can you see anything?" Lord Carnarvon asked, anxiously. Archaeologist Howard Carter was peering through a tiny hole, holding up a lighter. They had waited seven frustrating years for this moment. "Wonderful things," Howard Carter breathed.

A TEAM OF EXPERTS

Although Lady Evelyn Herbert, Lord Carnarvon's daughter, was the first to enter the tomb on that November day, the list of people involved in the opening of Tutankhamun's tomb reveals another truth: the sheer range of expertise Carter managed to enlist. There were 58 people present when he and Carnarvon first shone a light into Tutankhamun's resting place.

The multi-disciplinary team in this exemplary, scientifically planned project included philologist Sir Alan Gardiner, the Belgian archaeologist Jean Capart, the American archaeologist James Breasted, and John "Ora" Kinnaman, a Biblical scholar who would become the last remaining survivor of the Carter expedition, in 1961. The on-the-spot actions of chemist Alfred Lucas stabilized not just the grand chariots but the fragile linen gloves, wreaths of dried flowers, inscribed and painted boxes and chests crammed full of delicate fabrics, which would otherwise have fallen apart at a touch.

Cairo University's anatomist Douglas Derry analysed Tutankhamun's mummy, realizing from the stage of fusion of the trochanter and femur bones that the king was only 19 years old, while Sir Archibald Douglas Reid, an expert radiologist, X-rayed it, and Harry Burton photographed every find.

Unlike the tomb robbers who had gone before them, Carter's explorers were respectful, very conscious they were disturbing a Pharaoh's grave. Inside the sepulchral chamber, they found a low door, which gave way to another small room. In the centre of the room stood a shrine-shaped chest of pure gold with a goddess at each of its four corners. Their

THE CURSE OF KING TUT

The real story of the discovery of Tutankhamun's tomb is compelling enough, but add to that the so-called "curse", and you have true box office appeal. The Pharaohs' protective symbol was the cobra. On the day Carter opened the tomb, a cobra got into the cage of his pet canary and killed it. After that, no fewer than 20 people connected with the opening of the tomb seem to have died in mysterious circumstances. They included Lord Carnarvon, who died of an infected mosquito bite four months later; the Louvre's representative, Georges Bénédite, who succumbed to heat stroke; the young Egyptian Prince Ali Kamel Fahmy Bey, who was shot by his French wife of six months; and Carter's secretary Richard Bethell, who was found dead in his club in Mayfair, the victim of a suspected smothering. These deaths and others gave rise to the story that has dogged Egyptian archaeology ever since.

arms stretched out from the darkness as if in pleading. There was such an emotional charge in their expressions that the whole party was moved: "I am not ashamed to confess," wrote Carter, "that the sight brought a lump to my throat."

THE TOMB'S CONTENTS

Once Carter and his team had made their way down the stairs to Tutankhamun's tomb, they were faced with a corridor which led to an antechamber. There, they found what was described as "organized chaos", artefacts scattered all around due mostly to an unsuccessful attempt to rob the tomb.

The burial chamber, off which there were also a Treasury room and an annexe, held four wooden shrines that surrounded Tutankhamun's sarcophagi. The king had three sarcophagi, placed one inside the other. The outermost was of rose granite and yellow quartzite; the middle showed a painted scene of the young Pharaoh in ceremonial dress. The innermost sarcophagus was made of pure polished gold inlaid with green feldspar, cornelian, and lapis lazuli. The wonderful final effigy took the form of a golden mask covering head and shoulders, its eyes set in aragonite and obsidian.

In total, some 5,398 objects were catalogued by Carter and his team, and it took them ten years to do so. It was only in 2007 that Tutankhamun's mummy was finally returned to the tomb in the Valley of the Kings, where it is now on display.

OPPOSITE ABOVE
The boy king's stunning funeral mask.

OPPOSITE BELOW
Howard Carter (centre, with Lady Evelyn) and his team. Lord Carnarvon stands nearby holding a walking stick.

BELOW
A funerary boat, believed to carry the Pharaoh to the afterlife.

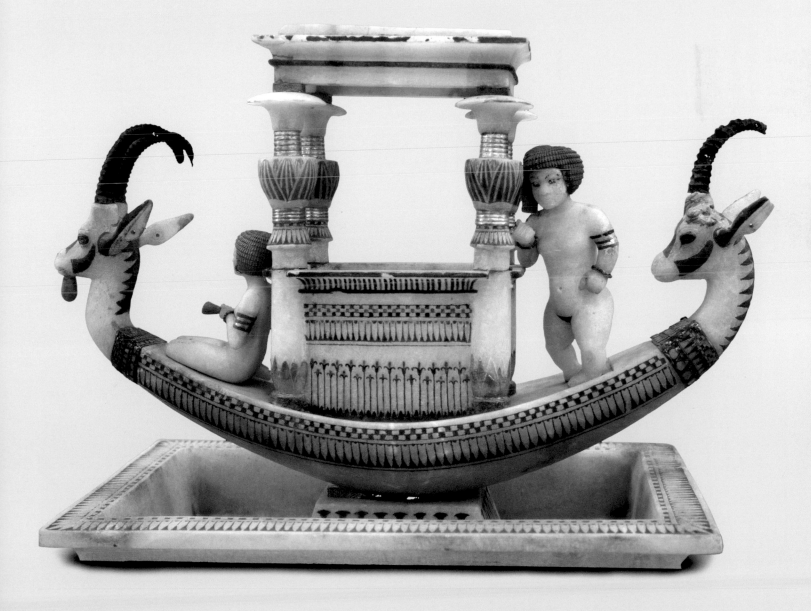

In 1995, excavating underneath an area Carter had blocked with some debris, US archaeologist Kent Weeks discovered a hidden entrance, just 3½ ft (110 cm) wide. Inside, he expected to find a handful of chambers, but instead found himself in a vast labyrinth of underground hallways. Built by Ramesses II, who ruled Egypt from 1279 BCE, the tomb (known as KV5) is utterly unique – the only royal "family tomb" in the Valley of the Kings.

Some researchers believe that Ramesses had more than 100 children: it's known for certain that he had 40 sons by his "primary" wives, as opposed to his concubines and slaves. Weeks and his

LEFT
Auguste Mariette, the man who set up the Egyptian Museum in Cairo.

BELOW
Part lion, part human: the awe-inspiring Great Sphinx of Giza. The pyramids of Menkaure and Khafre lie in the background.

fellow archaeologist, his wife Susan, have so far discovered 130 chambers at KV5.

Weeks is the director and founder of the magnificent Theban Mapping Project, which is working to improve – among many other things – the environmental conditions in tombs. Extremes of daily heat and nightly cold, combined with the moisture caused by the breath of thousands of tourists, are causing the exposed paint to peel off many tomb walls.

A MATTER OF LIFE AND DEATH

Each Pharaoh was seen as the progeny of the sun god who, with each reign, re-established order in a chaotic

universe. Even now, Egyptian history is conventionally divided into the Old, Middle and New Kingdoms, divided by periods of supposed chaos.

Preserving the earthly body of god-kings like Ramesses II and Tutankhamun, was essential: at stake was the continued wellbeing of Egypt. Once dead, the Pharaoh could communicate the needs of the people to the gods – so their mortuary shrines were intended to last. This, and the long series of spells known as *The Book of the Dead*, has given us a slightly distorted view, as if the ancient Egyptians spent their whole lives preparing for death.

Yet everyday Egypt was much more than morbid mummies and gloomy tombs. After two centuries of study, archaeologists are beginning to understand the culture more as a whole,

ABOVE
The mysterious tomb KV5, hidden in the Valley of the Kings.

BELOW
Taking the mickey?
A craftsman casts the Pharaoh as a mouse.

QUEEN NEFERTITI

Her name means "the beautiful one has come". Nefertiti was Akhenaten's favourite wife, famed for her beauty. The naturalism of this magnificent sculpture, made by the sculptor Thutmose *c.*1345 BCE, has made it a world-famous Egyptian icon. Yet it is uncharacteristic of most other Egyptian art. Thutmose's new creative freedom came from the artistic revolution that accompanied Akhenaten's extraordinary religious revolution. When the "Heretic Pharaoh" decided to replace the traditional worship of many gods with a cult of a single god, the Aten, or sun disc, Nefertiti was at his side. They moved the entire Egyptian court to a new capital, Amarna. Three and a half thousand years later, the archaeologist Ludwig Borchardt found the bust during the first German excavation of the site. Borchardt hid the queen from Egyptian officials, and Nefertiti turned up in Berlin in 1925, causing a huge scandal.

and less as a sequence of Pharaohs and artefacts. We've even found examples of working class humour. In one illustration excavated from the artist's village of Deir el-Medina, a craftsman drew a cartoon mouse Pharaoh sitting in a chariot. He attacks a citadel of cats, a parody of the official art he had to produce by day in the Valley of the Kings.

In a painting on the east wall of the tomb of Paheri, in the wine region of El Kab, a woman is depicted demanding 18 cups of wine: "For I wish to drink until drunkenness; my inside is like straw." There were many ancient wine factories in Egypt. Wine had sacred power, signifying eternity because it gave new life to those who drank it… historians tell us that during the Festival of Bastet, even the cat god got drunk.

WOMEN'S WORK

Women had a far more equal role than the (mostly male) 19th-century

OPPOSITE ABOVE
Imposing cliffs in the Valley of the Kings.

OPPOSITE BELOW
The bust of Queen Nefertiti.

ABOVE
The east wall of the tomb of Paheri depicting a woman in the middle of the bottom line ordering wine in order to get drunk.

archaeologists believed. Merneith, Khentkawes, Neithikret, Sobekneferu – there were many female rulers, including the famous Cleopatra of the later Ptolemaic dynasty, as well as influential consorts such as Queen Nefertiti, and we also know of two women viziers.

When female mummies with tattoos on their bodies were first discovered, most Egyptologists assumed they were women of low status, probably prostitutes or "dancing girls". Excavating ordinary village sites, William Flinders Petrie unearthed many sets of needles and dyes, indicating that commoners decorated their bodies. Yet the most famous of the tattooed female bodies was found in the tomb of a high-status official at Deir el-Bahari, normally an exclusively royal burial site.

Discovered in 1891 by the French Egyptologist Eugène Grébaut, Amunet was first thought to be a courtesan. She lived during Dynasty XI (c.2134–1991 BCE). Tattooed on the middle of her right thigh was a design of multiple diamond shapes; patterning her stomach are suggestively drawn circles, with undeniably carnal overtones. Amunet was a priestess of the sacred fertility goddess Hathor, and her story is part of the growing evidence that in ancient Egypt sexuality was intimately bound up with sacred ritual. It represented the link between the human and the divine: Nut, the sky goddess, was believed to swallow the sun each night and give birth to it the next morning.

MORE TO UNCOVER

Nearly a century after Howard Carter, Egyptology is experiencing another Golden Age. Advances in sensing technology are driving this new wave of archaeology. In 2016, a 7,000-year-old "lost city" was unearthed near Sohag. In March 2017, part of a statue (possibly of Ramesses II) was discovered in the Matariya district of Cairo and in April, news came of the location of a new pyramid just north of Sneferu's bent pyramid in the Dahshur necropolis south of Cairo. The story of ancient Egypt continues….

LEFT
The goddess Nut holds up the sky at the tomb of Horemheb, who reigned c.1348–1320 BCE.

BELOW
In 2017 a quartzite colossus of Ramesses II was discovered at ancient Heliopolis in Cairo.

THE MYSTERY OF THE INDUS

The urban-based civilization that arose along the banks of the Indus River, running across what today is northwest India and Pakistan, was the third to develop in the Ancient World. It would become the largest of all, at its peak extending over 600,000 square miles (1 million sq km). Emerging from about 2800 BCE, and fully formed from about 2500 BCE, at its peak the civilization comprised as many as 100 towns, as well as many substantial cities including Dholavira, Lothal, and the civilization's two largest and most dominant, Mohenjo-Daro and Harappa. And yet, for all its sweep, the Indus Valley culture suddenly suddenly began to decline around 1900 BCE.

BELOW
The ruins of Harappa, one of the largest cities of the Indus Valley civilization.

It was made possible by the 1,800-mile (3,000-km)-long Indus river and its tributaries, which run across the otherwise arid wastes of a vast plain between Baluchistan, mountainous and hostile, to the west, and the Thar Desert to the east. From here, the Indus flows into the Arabian Sea. Like the Nile, the Indus floods every spring, though in the case of the Indus it occurs as a result of melting Himalayan snow. The resulting irrigation and rich alluvial silts these floods provided created a narrow but fertile strip that naturally lent itself to settlement, giving rise to an astonishingly successful society, known as the Indus Valley Civilization or Harappan. Its development parallelled those of Mesopotamia, Egypt and China, producing a society that was literate, organized and, above all, urban.

Agriculture was nonetheless its bedrock. Wheat and barley, sown in the spring and requiring minimal attention, were the chief crops, though peas, too, were grown, and in some areas, especially further east, rice. Cotton is known to have

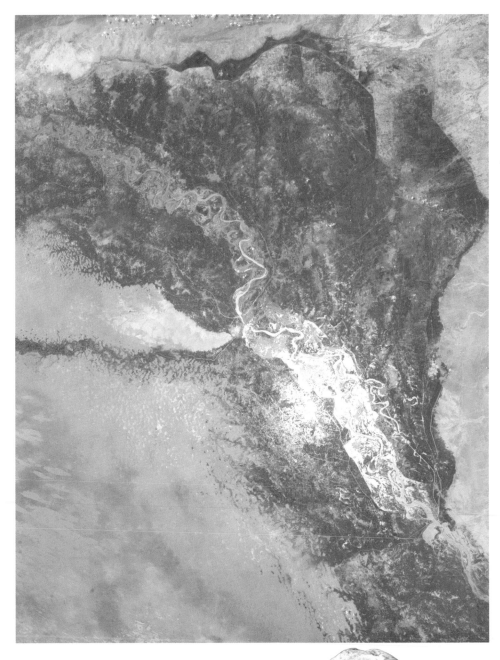

been cultivated and woven for clothes. Among those animals most successfully domesticated were cattle, sheep, goats, boars and elephants. Camel, too, may have been used. Whether as a food source or as beasts of burden, camels, too, were essential in the success of this new world.

DISCOVERING A NEW CIVILIZATION

Not the least remarkable aspect of the Indus Valley cities is the fact that, in striking contrast to the first cities of Mesopotamia, China and Egypt, until the 19th century it was a world whose existence was entirely unknown. It wasn't until the 1830s that a British adventurer and one-time soldier, Charles Masson, discovered Harappa, the first of many Indus Valley sites. Masson had little idea of its significance, and it was only after 1924 that the first excavations of the Indus Valley sites began at Mohenjo-Daro, discovered in 1920 by the leading Indian archaeologist of the time, R. D. Banerji.

A team from the Archaeological Survey of India led by K. N. Dikshit undertook these first investigations. Further work was carried out under a team led by British archaeologist John Marshall in 1925. Work on the site continued in the 1930s, conducted by the most noted archaeologist of the period, the flamboyant Mortimer Wheeler, director of the Indian Archaeological Survey between 1944 and 1948. Excavation resumed in 1945,

ABOVE
The Indus river flows nearly 2,000 miles (3,220 km) from its source in Tibet to the Arabian Sea.

RIGHT
This sculpture of a wild sheep is characteristic of the art style of Harappan culture.

THE CITY OF STONE

Thanks to its immense stone-built reservoirs, Dholavira is perhaps the most impressive Indus Valley site of all. The city was only discovered in 1968 and first excavated in 1989 by a team from the Archaeological Survey of India led by R. S. Bisht. Given the paucity of information about the Indus Valley cities, the results of the dig have added enormously to our knowledge of the period, and suggest that so large and precisely built a city could only have been the result of concerted central direction. The objects discovered include pottery, bronze, jewellery, terracotta statuary, a series of seals and, at ten characters in length, the longest continuous segment of the Indus script ever found.

Dholavira presents an even more compelling case for the sophistication of the Indus Valley. Whereas both Mohenjo-Daro and Harappa were built almost exclusively of baked bricks, Dholavira was built of stone. This reflects both the availability of stone as a building material and highlights a remarkable degree of centralized organization and technical capability.

The city's most impressive features are its 16 stone-built reservoirs, the largest 260 ft (79 m) long and 12 ft (7 m) deep. These indicate that the Indus Valley's civilization's management of water was exceptional.

In a region where several years might pass without rain, Dholavira created a

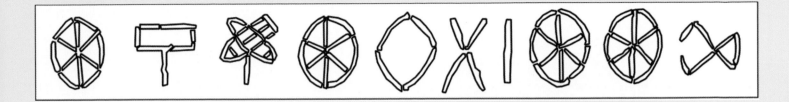

ABOVE
The ten characters found on the gate at Dholavira are the
longest continuous segment of Indus script ever discovered.

BELOW
Wells like this one were crucial to the survival of
Dholavira, located in a region where water was scarce.

vast system, using dams and resevoirs to assiduously collect and store both the river and rainwater that was vital to its prosperity.

At the heart of Dholavira there was a well, 13 ft (4 m) across and 65 ft (20 m) deep, lined with precisely engineered masonry. Its importance was plainly more than merely practical: it made very clear that water was, as has been said, "the mother of civilization".

reaching a peak in the mid-1960s with a team lead by an American archaeologist, George Dales. Further work was then suspended as anxieties grew about damage caused by the weathering of the structures exposed by the digs. In 2015, however, work was resumed under the aegis of Pakistan's National Fund for Mohenjo-Daro, which used the less damaging technique of dry core drilling. First results suggested that the site was very much larger than initially believed, even if its exact size remains a matter of speculation today.

AN UNKNOWN SOCIETY

For all of the excavation work, the Indus Valley's systems of government, religion and social organization today remain tantalizingly little known. No one can say if there were kings, nor even if a kind of single proto-state existed. The role of religious leaders, if any, remains equally elusive.

The simple reason for this is that there is no single substantial written record has come to light. Even so, this was a literate civilization: more than 3,500 individual inscriptions have been found on pottery, on clay seals, on bronze vessels and on fragments of ivory. At least 400 different symbols have been identified. Without a more substantial manuscript, the so-called Indus Valley Script remains undeciphered. Experts believe the language may belong

ABOVE TOP
Mohenjo-Daro was the first Indus Valley site to be excavated.

ABOVE
Sir Mortimer Wheeler (right), the flamboyant director of the Indian Archaeological Survey, with renowned archaeologist Louis Leakey.

OPPOSITE
This bust is of a king or a priest, but little is known about the Indus Valley's system of government.

to the Dravidian group and is a very distant ancestor of today's Tamil and Malayalam.

Despite the absence of any written record, the archaeological record, while incomplete, has revealed a well-ordered society of exceptional sophistication and reach. At its peak, the 99 acres (40 hectares) Mohenjo-Daro site is estimated to have had a population of 40,000. The city was laid out on a regular grid pattern, its main street never less than 30 ft (9 m) wide. A central citadel is thought to have been a religious, ceremonial and administrative hub.

One of Mohenjo-Daro's most startling feature is the 40 ft (12m) long, 13 ft (7m) wide and 11 ft (3 m) deep "Great Bath". Its purpose may have been purely sanitary – the city boasted 80 public lavatories as well as a complex system of sewers and drains: similarly, every house had its own well. But it may also have had a ritual function as a place of purification, with

ABOVE
An example of a stamp seal from the Indus Valley. Stamp seals were used to mark an item to show ownership and as a display of status.

water as the great cleanser and healer. In much the same way, it has been suggested that the adjoining "College Building" was home to a priestly caste.

A series of residential districts spread out from this central core. In some, the airy, flat-roofed houses were large and built around courtyards. Most inhabitants, though, lived in single-room dwellings, a series almost of tenements. The fact that in almost every Harappan settlement except Dholavira, the bricks used are of exactly the same size: 9 in x 5 in x 3 in (24 cm x 14 cm x 7 cm) is a further indicator of centralized social organization. A series of granaries provided storage for the region's agricultural products. As in the case of many other ancient civilizations, most of the clay seals so far discovered in the Indus Valley record financial transactions.

One of the earliest mysteries of the Indus Valley civilization was the discovery of a series of sites found to the east of the Indus river in a region that today is unremittingly hostile desert. How could these sites have been established with no ready access to water? The answer, simply,

is that there once was water, supplied by a river, the Ghaggar, similarly fed by melting Himalayan snows, whose course may have been catastrophically diverted by what is presumed to have been an earthquake. All that remains above ground today is a series of unpromising salty and stagnant pools. In fact, the river still flows underground; its surprise rediscovery in 1990 has transformed the region.

Built along the Sabarmati River on the Gulf of Khambhat, Lothal was discovered in 1954. Excavated by the Archaeological Survey of India between 1955 and 1960, the city was a gateway to the Indus civilization. Artefacts show it was a key link in the maritime trade routes that connected the Indus Valley with the wider world. It houses the oldest purpose-built dock yet found. The impressive dock also boasted a lock with wooden gates, designed to counter and exploit the substantial tidal range of the Gulf of Khambhat, allowing access at all times.

AN INDUSTRIAL INDUS

Able to barter a stable food supply for raw materials, above all copper and bronze, a series of thriving proto-industries developed in the region. Along with essentials such as pottery, a wide range of goods was produced: weapons, mirrors, jewellery, ceramics and even razors. These were traded to Persia and Afghanistan, hauled overland by bullock carts, the prime means of transport in the region.

Indus Valley sailors also pioneered maritime routes, taking advantage of the monsoon winds of the region. In 2,300 BCE, Sargon, the ruler of Agade in Mesopotamia, recorded the arrival of ships from the Indus Valley. By the end of the 3rd millennium BCE, the Indus Valley were at the centre of a great trading network that straddled the

Indian Ocean, central Asia and what would later be known as the Silk Road.

The steady accumulation of the archaeological evidence suggests that the Indus Valley was among the most dynamic civilizations of the Ancient World. Its influence on the later development of India is plain. It is possible, too, that the origins of Hinduism, the world's oldest religion, lie here: Hindu means "of the Indus".

No very compelling reasons have been offered to explain why the Indus Valley civilization ended so abruptly. It may have been the result of a change in the course of Indus river itself, which rendered once fertile regions barren. Climate change has also been suggested. All that can be said with certainty is that a vigorous and thriving society was brought to a more or less sudden end.

Yet its enduring significance cannot be overstated: the world that was never less than uncertain, the Indus Valley was the site of one of the first civilizations that transformed the way we live, replacing the hunter-gatherer lifestyle with settled agricultural and industrial societies. Farming based on the Indus River permitted the development of new, urban-based ways of life which in turn allowed the development of élites.

Much as the collapse of the society of the Mediterranean and the Levant towards the end of the 2nd millennium BCE was followed by a kind of dark age about which little can be said, the collapse of the Indus Valley civilization between 1900 and 1700 BCE was followed by a long gap in the archaeological and historical record.

It may have been filled c.1500 BCE by the arrival of Aryan peoples migrating from the northwest, although again, there is no indisputable no evidence of this. Wherever they came from and however much they may have exploited and learned from what remained of the Harappan world, they would be the next vital influence on the development of India.

THE VALLEY OF THE HUANG HE RIVER

Uniquely among the world's great civilizations, China can claim an unbroken line of descent from its first major civilization, the Shang, to the present. Culturally, linguistically, economically and politically, Shang China established a common Chinese identity that has endured for close to 4,000 years, despite periodic, convulsive and hugely destructive crises, natural and manmade. It represents an astonishing continuity. With the emergence of Shang China, by about 1800 BCE, China laid claims to levels of technical sophistication and social organization unmatched by Western civilizations for centuries.

As with the other civilizations of the ancient world, it was a river valley, in this case the Yellow River watercourse in north-central China, that made this transformation possible. It built on a much earlier agricultural transformation, as hunter-gatherers gradually developed settled agriculture, based on millet in the north of the country and based on rice in the south. Similarly, animals were domesticated, pigs and sheep in particular. Yet despite the development of a written script from about 1400 BCE, one that remains the basis of written

ABOVE
A depiction of the Yellow River, gave birth to civilization in China, by the artist Ma Yuan (1160–1225).

ABOVE
The Xianren Cave in Jiangxi Province.

RIGHT
Reconstructions of scenes inside the
Xianren Cave can now be seen by visitors.

Chinese today, the archaeological record has still proved critical in understanding how China under the Shang and later dynasties was formed. It has made clear a society of exceptional sophistication, disposing of no less exceptional resources

China was first settled by early hominids perhaps 500,000 years ago.

Homo sapiens seems to have become established there as early as 30,000 years ago. A cave dwelling in Jiangxi Province, the Xianren Cave, excavated in the 1990s, has produced evidence not just of early rice cultivation but of the earliest pottery ever found, dating from around 20,000 years ago.

SOCIETAL DEVELOPMENT

The transition from these early societies
to the vastly more sophisticated, urban-
based world of the Shang was never clear
cut. But when it came, the emergence
of a literate, highly stratified, technically
accomplished warrior civilization was
astonishing. It marked, too, the birth
of the Bronze Age in China, a point
highlighted by the increasing production
of bronze-cast objects, many exceptionally
intricate and elaborate.

The political complexion of Shang
China is uncertain. Was it a centralized
state ruling over much of northern China
from its various capitals, six in all, along
the Yellow River valley? Or was it, as
seems more probable, a more loosely
organized confederation of essentially
clan-based domains? The best evidence for
it comes from two sources: oracle bones
and those Shang tombs that have been
excavated.

Together, they highlight another
fundamental fact of Shang China: that
religion, which mostly took the form of
ancestor worship, a cult deemed worthy
only of the aristocracy, seems to have been
a private matter. There can be little doubt
that a priestly élite existed: oracle bone
divination would have been impossible

without it. Yet the kind of substantial
temples found in Mesopotamia and Egypt
seem not to have existed.

THE GRAVE OF FU HAO

The Shang tombs have made very clear
not just the importance of religion in
Shang China but the astonishing riches
that were lavished on it. The most
important of these tombs are in Yinxu.

ABOVE LEFT
Pottery from the neolithic village of Pan-p'o-ts'un from
4800 BCE.

OPPOSITE
A bronze ritual set from the Zhou dynasty.

Even if what is presumed to have been their exceptionally rich contents were mostly subsequently looted, what remains makes vividly clear the reach and potency of Shang China. In 1976, an unlooted tomb was found. It is the grave of Fu Hao, one of the wives of the Shang king Wu Ding, thought to have died in about 1200 BCE. If hardly on the startling scale of the 3rd century BCE tomb of the great Qin emperor Shi Huangdi and his terracotta army of 6,000 soldiers (see pages 71–4), it nonetheless contained 755 jade objects, 564 bone objects (500 hairpins among them), 468 bronze objects, 63 stone objects, 11 pieces of pottery, 5 ivory objects and 6,900 cowrie shells, then used as a form of currency. Also found were the skeletons of six dogs and 16 ritually sacrificed humans. This indicated a highly stratified society.

By about 1030 BCE, Shang rule had been overthrown, replaced by the Zhou, an ethnic group from northwest China.

ORACLE BONES

Shang oracle bones were first found in 1899 in the most important Shang archaeological site yet discovered, Yinxu, today in the modern city of Anyang. Their significance was first realized by the director of the Imperial College, Wang Yirong. By 1917, they had been deciphered by another Chinese scholar, Wang Guowei. It was he who realized that their script, part phonetic, part pictographic, was essentially unchanged in modern Chinese. Oracle bones were generally the shoulder bones of a beast of burden, typically water buffalo or cattle, that were heated until they cracked. The resulting cracks were then interpreted or divined by a seer, the result recorded in writing on the bone itself. Such divinations could cover almost any subject, from the weather to major military campaigns. However brief their texts, they are an essential window into the world of Shang China.

The Zhou dynasty presents an obvious paradox. In the first place, the centralized authority of the Shang was abandoned in favour of a series of domains, almost like European fiefdoms, awarded to those loyal to the Zhou. But in 771, the majority of these feudal territories broke away from the Zhou, becoming in effect independent during the Spring and Autumn period. Almost 100 such rival states appeared. The Zhou, with their power greatly reduced, became

ABOVE
An oracle bone inscribed with ideograms.

BELOW
The tomb of Fu Hao.

ABOVE
The Kang Hou *gui*, a ritual bronze urn.

merely one among them. It was a process accompanied by almost constant warfare. The years between 472 and 221 BCE, when these numerous petty states were reduced to 20, as conquest on a startling scale occurred, were aptly named the Warring States period.

But whatever its political fragmentation, whatever the consequences of centuries of brutal warfare, China itself, in the sense of an area that became recognizably Chinese culturally, was enormously extended. By the 5th century BCE the Yangtze valley to the south and much of Manchuria to the north had been definitively integrated into this Chinese cultural world. At the same time, significant technological advances were made and many Chinese political institutions reformed and strengthened.

By the 4th century BCE, the leading Chinese states commanded armies whose combined numbers approached one million. Some battles saw in excess of 100,000 men deployed. Warfare on this scale was unknown in any other part of the world. In Europe it wouldn't be matched until the 16th century.

A New Level of Craftsmanship

At the same time, levels of craftsmanship reached new heights. As early as the 11th century BCE, at the start of the Zhou dynasty, bronze workers were capable of works as refined as the Kang Hou *gui* or urn, a ritual food vessel. (The urn is important, too, as evidence of Zhou

feudal grants of territory: an inscription around its lip records that territories in Wey were granted to Kang Hou, the Marquis of Kang, brother of King Wu, for his suppression of a Shang rebellion.)

From *c.*650 BCE, iron began to be used for the first time. From the 5th century BCE, as stone and bone tools were increasingly replaced by iron implements, agricultural production was hugely boosted. The introduction of coins, widely circulated by the 4th century BCE, was similar evidence of growing economic sophistication.

The technological prowess of China in this otherwise tumultuous period is very well illustrated by the Tonglushan mine, discovered in Hubei province in 1973 and excavated over the following 12 years. The excavations revealed a site that was genuinely a kind of proto-industrial complex, in continuous use for 1,000 years from about 700 BCE. Several hundred mining shafts, originally lined by bamboo, were discovered along with a series of smelting furnaces and around 1,000 mining tools. Evidence for sophisticated ventilation systems was found. Methods for removing ground-water also came to light during excavation. The complex covered an area of some 20 acres (9 hectares). It is estimated that 80,000 tons of copper was produced here, all of it by hand.

It was exactly this kind of technological and organizational superiority, combined with an ever-stronger sense of a unified Chinese identity, that would make China so formidable a force when, in 221 BCE, it was forcibly re-united under the single rule of the Qin emperor Shi Huangdi.

RIGHT
The Tonglushan mine was an ancient industrial complex consisting of hundreds of mining shafts and furnaces.

CLASSICAL &
EARLY CIVILIZATIONS
IN EUROPE

CLASSICAL GREECE

High society was obssesed with the virtues of Classical Greece. In the 18th century, aristocrats from across Europe flocked to Greece as part of the "Grand Tour". At the same time, academia began to argue about the nature of its famed democracy and philosophy.

Finding the site of Olympia, ancient Greece's most important religious, sporting and political centre, was a sort of Holy Grail for European antiquarians. The ancient Greeks had celebrated their great athletes by commissioning bronze and marble statues, and the experts believed they would find "wonderworks by the thousand" if they could discover the site where the ancient Olympics were held.

By 1723, antiquarians such as the French scholar Bernard de Montfaucon had spent many years trying to identify the site. In fact, most of Olympia's largest statuary had already been looted in antiquity by the Romans, including the famed gold and ivory statue of Zeus, the king of the gods, carved by the great sculptor Phidias.

In 1766, the British Society of Dilettanti commissioned a young architect called Richard Chandler to try and find it. After three long years of wandering, he discovered some likely looking ruins in the wild mountains of the Peloponnese, hidden in an overgrown vineyard. It wasn't until 1829, however, that the French excavated the site, uncovering the Temple of Zeus. As was by now traditional, they shipped the finest pieces of sculpture back to the Louvre.

PREVIOUS PAGES
A Roman mosaic from Ephesus.

OPPOSITE ABOVE LEFT
The monk Bernard de Montfaucon began a craze for
publishing books about "Antiquity" in the 18th century.

OPPOSITE BELOW
This Ionic temple erected at Olympia by Philip II of
Macedonia marked the victory of 338 BCE.

ABOVE
The Lion Gate of Mycenae.

This prompted a fiery correspondence
with Greeks inspired by the ideals of the
French revolution. Why shouldn't those
ideals of freedom, of ownership by the
people, for the people, apply to them?

The Greek Archaeological Service was
set up in 1833, immediately after Greece
established its independence from the
Ottoman Empire, under the control of
the Ministry of Culture. However, the
feverish interest from western European
countries was such that many institutions
were established throughout the middle
and latter part of the 19th century, with
the French School at Athens being the
first in 1846.

Eventually, it was the Germans who
were given exclusive rights to excavate

Olympia, under a team led by Friedrich
Adler, Richard Bohn and Ernst Curtius.
They were assisted by Wilhelm Dörpfeld,
whose work at Mycenae and with
Heinrich Schliemann on the site of Troy
would make him one of the leading
archaeologists of Bronze Age sites. He
later revealed the Hekatompedon temple
at the Acropolis in Athens.

Greece became an inspiration for
academics, artists and writers alike: the
poet Byron set off for Messolonghi, a
hub of the Greek War of Independence,
where he died of a fever in 1824. Every
night, the future Ludwig I of Bavaria read
aloud from his original Greek version of
the Gospels, a bust of Homer by his side.
The philosopher Wilhelm Traugott Krug

This is a funeral mask made for a king of kings. It's also one of the most powerful and compelling archaeological discoveries of all time. The thin, haughty face, portrayed in beaten gold with astonishing naturalism, is on display in the National Archaeological Museum of Athens. The man who supposedly lay in death beneath this golden mask is one of the strongest but darkest characters in ancient Greek literature. Impatient, and quick to anger, Agamemnon was the quarrelsome, stubborn and arrogant leader of the Achaeans, who massed against Troy. So that he could win in battle, he sacrificed his own daughter. When he returned from war triumphant, his wife murdered him. The only problem is that this is not Agamemnon. The shaft graves where this treasure was found date from 1600 BCE, 300 years before Homer's account of the Trojan War.

tried to establish "Philhellene" societies, supporting volunteers who would travel in the Greek – and Christian – cause. The three great German poets Goethe, Schiller and Hölderlin might have lived and breathed in Germany, but the mainstay of their poetic imaginations was Greece.

Schliemann's work at Troy and Mycenae fuelled the public's interest. His discovery of "Priam's Treasure" (see page 48) and the so-called "Mask of Agamemnon", were extremely newsworthy.

Around the same time as Dörpfeld and Schliemann were at work, so the new Keeper of the Ashmolean Museum in Oxford, Arthur Evans, began to plan one of the greatest excavations ever to take place in Greece, on the island of Crete.

A devoted scholar, Evans was the complete antithesis of Schliemann. Still, he had keenly followed the debate about whether Homer's "Troy" could really be a genuine city, as opposed to the figment of a poetic mind. Evans had even visited Schliemann on site. Like Schliemann, he was a wealthy man. Once he heard tales of exquisite antiquities being dug up on the island, there was no holding him back. By chance, Evans had got hold of some strange golden seal-stones in an Athens flea market. Amulet-sized and beautifully

engraved, they were decorated with an unknown, pictographic script. He had a hunch that the strange writing was evidence of an entire lost civilization waiting to be discovered.

The fact that Crete was embroiled in a war did not stop him. As a result of his journalistic support for the island's fledgling republic, Evans secured the sole rights of excavation at the place he had set his sights on: the Kafala Hill. After Crete had won its independence, Evans used an inheritance to purchase the site in 1900. What he discovered there would be a sensation (see pages 140–1).

Evans spent his life devoted to Knossos, although he also played a key part in the development of both the Ashmolean and the British Museum.

ABOVE
The Mask of Agamemnon.

RIGHT
Sir Arthur Evans.

THE RAVAGES OF WAR

You don't need to be a specialist to
know how much damage can be done
to a precious site by an invading or
occupying army: the deliberate and
systematic destruction of the Warsaw
ghetto by the Nazis in World War II is
one horrific example. The nearest miss
in archaeological history, though, has
to be the almost total destruction of the
Parthenon during the Great Turkish War
of 1683–89.

Even in its ruined state today, the
temple remains a symbol of civilization,
a hymn to the extraordinary aesthetic
and cultural accomplishments of Ancient
Greece. Yet it nearly wasn't so.

Possibly believing that the Venetian
commander Morosini would not attack
a building of such importance, the
occupying Turkish soldiers fortified the
Parthenon and used it to store their
gunpowder. They were sorely mistaken.
On 26 September 1685, a Venetian
mortar round scored a direct hit, and
blew up the gunpowder store. The titanic
explosion came very close to razing
the greatest example of Classical Greek
architecture ever built. The occupying
troops took to grinding up slabs of fallen
marble to make yet more gunpowder.

For the next 150 years, the building
endured further sporadic looting, until,
in 1801, the Earl of Elgin bought some
of the remaining sculptures and friezes,

THE LEGEND OF THE MINOTAUR

"Out in the middle of the wine-dark sea there is an island called Crete, a rich and lovely land, washed by the sea on every side... Among the ninety cities is Knossos, a great city; and there Minos was nine years king, the boon companion of mighty Zeus."

The Odyssey (Book 19) Homer

The *Iliad* and its counterpart the *Odyssey*, with their tales of epic heroism and impossibly beautiful women, were founding texts of Western civilization. Embedded in these Greek myths was an enticing idea: that once there had been a lost island, the true home of the gods of myth. Terrifying tales emerged from the island's mists: of Icarus, who flew too close to the sun; Theseus, who killed the grisly half-bull, half-man monster called the Minotaur, and the great king Minos who had fathered the monster, and kept him lurking in his labyrinth. According to myth, Zeus himself was born on Crete.

Evans's dig at Knossos began in March 1900. One day, one of the local workmen suddenly cried out in fear. He had found a "black devil" he shouted, shying away from the sinister head he had plucked out from the soil. A black, red-eyed bust of a bull's head, with huge, gilded curved horns and a rippled neck was staring back at him. Made out of precious stone and mother of pearl, the "rhyton" found that day is more than 3,500 years old.

The drama convinced Evans that he had found the true home of the mythical King Minos. More artefacts and fragments of frescoes told him that the people who had lived at Knossos worshipped the bull. The labyrinth of buildings emerging from the ground was truly ancient, older by far than Athens' magnificent Parthenon, built *c.*450 BCE when Classical Greece was at its height.

Evans had unearthed an entire, lost civilization, documented by many beautiful works of art. Frescoes depicted a sophisticated culture based on colour, dance, swimming, music, acrobatic bull-jumping and joy. The first level excavated dates from *c.*1900 BCE, but was built on the ruins of a settlement that was even older. Knossos was as ancient as the oldest Egyptian pyramids: contemporary with the time of the Egyptian Old Kingdom, 2575–2134 BCE.

The Bronze Age "palace" was monumental in size and scale, built using fine ashlar masonry. It held many shrines, and a Throne Room, with a red panel at the centre of the floor: a colour known to be associated with the underworld.

In what Evans called the "Hall of the Double Axes", a private chamber with an inner space closed off by 11 sets of double doors, he found the dissolved remains of what most experts agree was a throne. It rested not on a stone dais, but on four fluted wooden columns.

As find after find built up, including many tablets inscribed with an early form of writing, he realized that the lives of the inhabitants had been luxurious. The palace had running water, baths and even alabaster windows. Both women and men wore exotic jewellery and make up. Men wore ceremonial headdresses and flared kilts; for ceremonies, the women went bare-breasted. Knossos's magnificent frescoes were brilliant evidence of a highly-developed artistic culture, including the world's first naturalistic depictions of landscape.

There was also an underground sewage system, the world's first known flush toilet, and extensive storage magazines, still filled with the signs of vast commercial wealth. Most exciting for Evans was the discovery of the prehistoric script now known as Linear B, which was vivid proof of an advanced, cultured society, the hub of Mediterranean Bronze Age civilization.

This was a landmark excavation. Newspapers across the world trumpeted the exciting news.

Evans's assistant Duncan Mackenzie kept detailed daily records, while Evans was tireless in documenting his research. Yet Evans's approach, while flamboyant and eye-catching, was hasty, viewed from a modern perspective. He shoehorned preconceived ideas into the mix in a desperate attempt to force the evidence into shape. Those distinctive, primitive-looking, black-topped red columns which

ABOVE
A detail from a fresco in the Throne Room, Knossos.

BELOW
Evans's "reconstruction" is visually strong, but is it accurate?

are today the trademark of the site are built out of modern concrete and are part of Evans's "reconstruction". An educated guess, yes, but still a guess. Many years later it is hard to know what is original, and what is reconstructed. Scholars have to go back to the excavation records again and again to try and re-interpret what

Evans and Mackenzie originally found, and where.

Minoan archaeology has come a long way since. What Evans desperately wanted to interpret as the magnificent royal residence of King Minos seems in truth to have been a religious shrine, or temple. Although Knossos may have had a highly powerful leader, he – or she – was most likely a religious figure, a kind of "Solar Moon King". Ancient Minoans were just as often led by a priestess as a priest.

Ironically, although he was the first to discover the enigmatic scripts known as Linear A and B, Evans was never able to translate them. He spent the rest of his life trying.

Could the Minoans be the inspiration behind the myth of the lost city of Atlantis? In a fascinating story of its own, a new wave of archaeological and geological evidence suggests that Minoan civilization was struck by a devastating tsunami that triggered huge destruction. It hit Crete after a volcanic eruption on the island of Thera (now Santorini), by then part of the greater Minoan maritime empire.

LEFT
Amphiloplis has become
one vast excavation site.

BELOW
A bust of Hephaestion,
Alexander's possible lover.

presumed that he was buried in Egypt, and
without significant remains, it has been
impossible for archaeology to help resolve
the debate. Then, in 2012, a phenomenally
large tomb was uncovered on the Kasta
Hill at Amphipolis, in northern Greece, a
site close to the Aegean port that Alexander
used for his fleet. The tomb is enormous,
its massive perimeter wall, clad in dressed
marble from the island of Thassos, is 1,630
ft (497 m) long. Excavations of the entire
site will take many years.

Clearly, someone very important was
buried here. Excitement mounted as
evidence of a huge monument emerged.
Topped with a statue of a lion, it would
have been clearly visible from sea. So far,
only two years of excavation have been
funded. Excavators are attempting to
stabilize the tomb contents, rescuing the
paintings from the ravages of humidity.

Is this Alexander's tomb? Or was it built
for Hephaestion, Alexander's childhood
friend and lover? Like Alexander,
Hephaestion died suddenly, succumbing

to an unidentified ailment in 324 BCE, at
Ecbatana in Iran.

The lead archaeologist at Amphipolis,
Katerina Peristeri, is convinced that the
site began as a funerary monument for
Hephaestion: there is an inscription on one
wall that suggests that Alexander himself
commissioned it, and had it built between
325 and 300 BCE. There, though, the
certainties end. Owing to the work
of looters, the stratigraphy has been
destroyed, and most of the grave goods
have gone. Accelerator mass spectrometry,
[AMS] analysis may tell us more about the
bones, but the project as a whole will take
years to complete.

A NEVER-ENDING STORY

Greece has such a rich history that it
is difficult to imagine a more fertile
ground for archaeology. A team from the
University of Cincinnati uncovered the

grave of a man, now known as the Griffin Warrior, at the Palace of Nestor at Pylos. The remains of this Mycenean grandee were surrounded and covered by bronze, silver and gold objects, shedding light on his status and the funerary procedures of males of the period.

As recently as 2016, the remains of a 2,500-year-old city near the village of Vlochós, about five hours north of Athens, were discovered by a team of Swedish archaeologists from the University of Gothenburg.

LEFT
Alexander the Great.

BELOW
The tomb of the Griffin Warrior, found in an olive grove, held unprecedented treasures.

Relics of the Roman Empire

It is impossible to encapsulate a full thousand years of Roman history in one short chapter, but the story of the Emperor Caracalla, best known for his magnificent public baths, which were free to all and even included a library, has a special resonance in today's world.

In 212 CE, Caracalla decreed that wherever they lived, from Spain to Syracuse, from the British Isles to Egypt, every free inhabitant of the Roman Empire was a bona fide Roman citizen. Overnight, more than 30 million people from the provinces became legally Roman, which must qualify as the biggest offer of citizenship in world history.

To some eyes, this may seem strange, but the Romans had a unique way of appropriating the "other" as a way of preventing it from becoming dangerous. The cult of Cybele, an unexpected fruit

ABOVE
Roman emperors vied to produce the most spectacular public buildings. Caracalla's baths, completed 212–217 CE, were a marvel of engineering, bringing thermal spring water into the city via aqueducts.

LEFT
A Roman relief from the Medici villa.

| **753** BCE Rome is founded | **509** BCE Rome becomes a republic | **264** BCE Rome completes the conquest of Italy | **183** BCE Hannibal dies | **73–71** BCE Spartacus's Slave Rebellion | **58–52** BCE Julius Caesar conquers Gaul | **46** BCE Julius Caesar becomes dictator | **27** BCE Augustus becomes Emperor |

of Rome's expansion into Anatolia, was initially thought to be a subversive, even menacing, form of worship. Yet the mother goddess's temple ended up on the Palatine, the very heart of Rome. Recent studies have shown that, far from looking to diminish the cult and its power, Rome's first emperor, Augustus, raised the floors of the temple and substantially restored it.

FOUNDATIONS

In a city as well studied as this, it's surprising how much more there is to learn, but Rome never ceases to stun the world. According to legend, the twins Romulus and Remus founded Rome in the 8th century BCE. Romulus killed Remus in a dispute over which of them had the support of the gods. Modern archaeological technologies are opening up many new discoveries: employing auger-type probes more often used in engineering, archaeologists even believe they have located the twins' very first home, the "Lupercal cave", deep in the honeycomb core of the Palatine Hill.

In the 19th century, Giacomo Boni rediscovered an ancient iron-age shrine, the Lapis Niger. In Imperial Rome, it was said to be where Romulus met a grisly end, as members of the senate stabbed him to death. The records are unclear, but some describe the spot as a sacred part of the original Comitium, an early assembly place where rulers addressed the citizens.

Within the gloom of the buried temple, Boni found a mysterious inscribed stone, its writing running left to right, right to left, "as an ox would plough a field". This is the earliest Latin inscription ever found. No one has ever completely deciphered it, but one word does clearly stand out: "Rex" (king).

Augustus's famous Forum Romanum was built around and above this sacred space, which it has long been suspected holds the key to the foundation of

ABOVE
Lost, but now found? A she-wolf raised Rome's foundling fathers in the Lupercal Cave.

LEFT
The mysterious Lapis Niger stele.

27 BCE	60/61 CE	83 CE	117 CE	212 CE	325 CE	410 CE	476 CE
The Roman Empire begins	Boudicca's Revolt	Agricola completes conquest of Britain	The Roman Empire is at its height	Freemen of the Roman Empire are given citizenship	Constantine adopts Christianity	The Visigoths attack Rome	The western Roman Empire ends and Ancient Rome falls

The Forum: centre of commercial and religious life throughout the Republic and the most celebrated meeting place in the world. It was half-buried under sediment until Italian abbot and antiquities specialist Carlo Fea began to dig out the Arch of Septimius Severus in 1803.

BELOW
The Pantheon, unique in that it seems to have been dedicated to all the gods, not just one. Built by Hadrian in the 2nd century CE, its huge dome was an engineering first. The interior's divine symmetry is flooded with light.

Rome itself. Recently, a team of Italian archaeologists used laser scanners and photography from historical excavations to pinpoint the oldest walls underground, and employed modern techniques to re-date the minute fragments of pottery and grains in the surrounding level. The team feels their evidence pushes the story of the Eternal City, and possibly even that of Romulus and Remus, back by several hundred years.

The feats of engineering, together with the beauty, ingenuity and durability of the buildings that the Romans created still continue to amaze us. These were a major contribution to civic life. In the provinces, the well-ordered city was the prime agent in spreading *Romanitas*, a sense of Rome's benefits and its values. In Rome, Caracalla's baths continued a long tradition of building on an Imperial and lavish scale: the Circus Maximus; Hadrian's magnificent villa; the Colosseum, built to stamp out memories of Nero's lavish personal fun palace, and the "Golden House". Rome was a city of gold, marble and bronze, but its chickpea-fed armies were tougher than old leather. Beyond its powerful walls and towers stretched the 1,931,000 square miles (5,000,000 sq km) of the empire. No one could have imagined that this great city would fall, but fall it did.

Two hundred years after Caracalla's death, in 410 CE, the Visigoths attacked and plundered the city. Over the centuries, the magnificent Forum

became first a field where farmers grazed their cattle and grew vines, and then a swamp crawling with toads and vipers. Cows drank in the fountains, and the Colosseum's expensive dressed stone became a quarry for the popes. Rome echoed to the calls of the night birds across the banks of the filthy river Tiber.

DIGITAL ROME

Rome is a multi-layered city, what scholars call a "palimpsest". For the first-time visitor, it can be a hard book to read. There's modern Rome, 18th-century Rome, Renaissance Rome. Then there's the Vatican, a city all to itself. And what of antiquity? The Emperor Augustus claimed to have turned this place from a city of brick into a city of marble; wouldn't it be wonderful to see the city as he did?

Since the Renaissance, artists, scholars, architects and – latterly – archaeologists have been trying to decipher the complex urban landscape of this city. Now, thanks to digital technology and a huge amount

of dedicated scholarship, everyone can enjoy the fruits of their labour.

The Roman Antiquities Service (*Forma Romae*) is making it possible to explore the megalopolis through interactive maps or in virtual reality, via 3D models online. It is concentrating on Augustan Rome for now, although in future, it hopes to cover other periods. It aims to create accurate archaeoscapes that one can "fly" through.

How accurate a vision is this? Archaeology proves our interpretation of history can't be fixed, but the new virtual views of Rome are not video games; they are as well informed as it is possible to be. An American project from the Universities of Arizona and Pennsylvania, Rome Reborn, focuses on specific aspects of the city, such as the magnificent Pantheon at the height of its glory. Dr Matthew Nicholls of the Classics Department at the University of Reading has created a digital model of the entire city – just as it would have been in the 4th century CE. In London, meanwhile, UCLA has created sophisticated digitized models with detailed "footnotes" on each building. Prepare to be amazed.

ABOVE
A digital recreation of the Circus Maximus in the 4th century. This was the first and largest chariot-racing stadium in Rome, but was also used for *ludi*, huge religious festivals.

THE COLOSSEUM

The Colosseum showed the Romans at their mightiest but also at their most cruel. Built in 72–80 CE, the poet Martial described it as the eighth wonder of the world; the height of Roman building technology. The stadium could even be flooded to stage naval battles or redecorated as a jungle, to entertain up to 50,000 spectators. Behind those serried ranks of magnificent arches, the Romans killed thousands of people, many of them Christians. A favourite trick was to put prisoners on seesaws, and then release starving lions from the basement trapdoors. To survive, a prisoner had to drive his or her end of the seesaw into the air and be responsible for the person opposite being mauled and eaten. *Damnatio ad Bestius* – the Condemnation of Beasts.

BELOW
Piranesi's engraving of the majestic building in which the Martyrs' cross can be seen in the middle.

BOTTOM
The Colosseum as it is today.

The magnificent building illustrates one of the dilemmas of archaeology: how far to dig? Which period should you destroy, in order to restore another? Ironically, the Colosseum's use as a place of Christian martyrdom is one reason why it survived. In 1874, when archaeologists began to excavate, they removed a medieval hermit and his hermitage, along with the black Martyrs' cross seen immortalized in the engravings of Piranesi. Christians came out in protest, to pray on the sacred ground where the Martyrs had suffered and died. Nowadays, it is possible to see the extent of the hypogeum, the labyrinth of passageways and cages that existed beneath the arena.

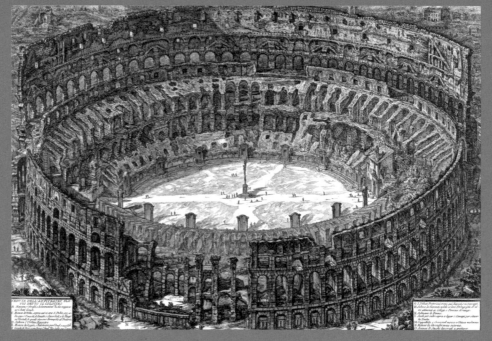

ABOVE
The extraordinary Pont Du Gard in southern France.

RIGHT
A detail from a column in Leptis Magna, Libya.

BEYOND ROME

Why was the Roman Empire so successful, and how did it last for some 500 years? Sheer ingenuity played a large part. A map of the empire at the height of its territorial expansion under Trajan and Hadrian would show domination of most of modern Europe; the north coast of Africa including Egypt; much of Turkey and the Middle East, and a big slice of what is now Russia. Both Trajan and Hadrian were actually born in Spain.

Unity was achieved by tight initial control, using a universally accepted currency, and investing heavily in engineering works and infrastructure such as water works and roads. The Romans accepted the different customs, religions and cultures of the people they conquered, eventually making many of them citizens.

Rome offered remarkable modernity. Its mark can still be seen in language, laws, architecture, engineering and government. Many of the landmarks they created had a formal beauty and, like Leptis Magna or the Pont du Gard in France, are now listed by UNESCO as World Heritage sites. We are even now making major new Roman finds, like the city of Ucetia recently found at Uzès, in the south of France.

PUTTING UP A FIGHT: THE ROMANS IN BRITAIN

The Romans invaded Britain under Emperor Claudius. In 43 CE, the empire was only a few decades old, but entering a period of unparalleled expansion. Would a few, obscure islands on the empire's north-western edges cause the super-efficient Romans any problems? Well, yes. While some British tribes were at odds with one another, which helped the Romans divide and rule, many put up stiff resistance, led at first by Togodumnus and Caratacus, sons of Cunobeline, King of the Catuvellauni.

BELOW
A fascinated crowd gathers in 1950s London to see what archaeologists would reveal about the Temple of Mithras.

Under Agricola's leadership between 78 and 84 CE, the Romans largely subdued the British, but rebellion against the invaders flared up repeatedly when he was recalled to Rome. Most notable was the revolt led by an alarmingly fierce, flame-haired Celt called Bouddica, queen of the Iceni.

Suetonius finally defeated Boudicca and her army at the Battle of Watling Street in 60 or 61 CE, but even so, Nero considered abandoning the Roman occupation of Britain altogether: too much trouble for too little gain. Boudicca's own fate is uncertain, although it's possible she took poison rather than surrender. For a society as patriarchal as ancient Rome, wrote the historian Dio, "the fact all this ruin was brought by a woman in itself caused them the greatest shame."

Fantastic tales abound that Boudicca is buried under Platforms 8, 9 or 10 in King's Cross Station. Burials from this time often leave no trace, especially when the death was in battle. Yet in 2012, as part of the London Crossrail project, archaeologists found a vast

number of simultaneously buried skeletons. This added to intriguing evidence already found around the Roman Temple of Mithras in the City of London, which was only uncovered because of enemy bombing during World War II.

The temple was excavated in 1954 by William Grimes, whose work was rushed by development pressure. Winston Churchill stepped in and extended the excavation time, after thousands of people flocked to see the dig. Eventually, some of the finest Roman sculptures found in Britain were recovered.

The recent re-development of a 3-acre (1.2-hectare) site for Bloomberg became a chance to reconstruct the Temple of Mithras underneath the office block at the exact spot it was built in 240 CE. Ground level in Roman London was 23 ft (7 m) below today's. London's single largest archaeological excavation, it revealed a bustling Roman street scene from the 1st century CE, as well as the long-buried river Walbrook.

The dig uncovered a large ceramic pot containing some ritually buried skulls, gold coins, amulets and pagan tokens. All had been wonderfully preserved for almost 2,000 years in the muddy riverbed. It is tempting to think of Boudicca and her warriors sending these along the stream as offerings to the gods, much like the wonderful Battersea Shield. This beautifully worked Celtic, La Tène bronze shield was dredged out of the rich Thames mud in 1857; archaeologists believe it was a votive offering, and it too was found with the remains of many Roman-era skeletons.

LEFT
Not Roman, but Celtic: the Battersea Shield.

BELOW
The great warrior queen and her daughters, as envisaged by sculptor Thomas Thorneycroft.

BOUDICCA

Tacitus tells us that in 60 or 61 CE, the Romans flogged Boudicca and publicly raped both her daughters when she objected to the Roman annexation of Iceni lands – in current day Norfolk. In response, Boudicca unleashed fury. The Iceni burned the Roman occupied towns of Camulodunum (Colchester) and Londinium to the ground, killing thousands in the process. Clear burn lines in the stratigraphy attest to this. At Colchester, digs have shown that every care was taken to destroy everything that was Roman. Even buildings of clay, which is very difficult to burn, were demolished brick by brick. Every "collaborator" the Iceni could find was hunted down and killed: experts liken it to a campaign of ethnic cleansing. Boudicca may also have burned Verulamium (St Albans), although there is less clear archaeological evidence for this.

VINDOLANDA

The Vindolanda tablets give the best insight into what it was like to be a Roman citizen or soldier living in a fort on the very edge of the Roman Empire. Hadrian's wall still separates England and Scotland. Before the wall was constructed, the earliest forts were entirely isolated. The first at Vindolanda was begun in 85 CE and finished by 92 CE. Most of the inscribed wooden tablets, which were ditched in a rubbish dump near the commander's *mansio*, or mansion, date from the period when the fort was enlarged, between 92 and 102 CE.

One tablet's dismissive description of the British makes it sound as if they remained an active enemy: "the Britons are unprotected by armour. There are very many cavalry. The cavalry does not use swords nor do the wretched little Britons mount in order to throw javelins." Yet many of the tablets give a sense of a relatively peaceful lifestyle. Perhaps the wall's primary purpose was not to keep out "savage barbarians", but to mark the limits of the empire as a political entity, and to levy taxes and customs duties?

In one well-known message, a centurion's wife, Claudia Severa, invites her sister, Lepidina, to a party. In another, an unknown soldier receives word of a care package: "I have sent you… pairs of socks from Sattua, two pairs of sandals and two pairs of underpants…." It sounds as if his mother – or his wife – was as worried about the British weather as she was about defending the wall.

The Bloomberg (Mithras) dig in London also unearthed an entirely new set of wooden tablets, even older than the ones at Vindolanda. Historically, one of the most important is a contract dated 22 October 62 CE for the transport of 20 wagonloads of provisions from St Albans to London. Tacitus dates Boudicca's rebellion to 61 CE, but if both St Albans and London were razed with enormous loss of life, it seems unlikely both cities could have bounced back quite so quickly. The tablet suggests that Boudicca's insurrection may well have taken place earlier. Whatever the exact truth, the

ABOVE
Remote Romans: Housesteads Roman fort, in the Northumbrian wilds.

ABOVE LEFT
One of the Roman writing tablets found in Vindolanda at Hadrian's Wall, this letter refers to supplies of wheat.

separate forms of material, archaeological and historical evidence, are an intriguing check and balance.

The Bloomberg tablets prove that this area of London has been a trading and financial hub since the earliest years of the Roman occupation. There are 405 tablets in total, many of them recording financial transactions.

The Western Roman Empire effectively came to an end in the 5th century CE, but Roman influence in Britain had been on the wane for more than a century before that. However, the empire's remarkable legacy both in Britain and throughout Europe, North Africa and the Near East was incalculable.

Lords of the North

With the fall of the Roman Empire, Europe entered a period of fragmentation, economic decline and frequent warfare known as the Dark Ages. As Roman authority collapsed, new powers rose to fill the vacuum. In northern Europe, the Norsemen of Scandinavia plundered, pillaged and colonized their neighbours at the same time as Christianity took root through much of the continent. Local kings and warlords sought to establish themselves as the natural successors to the fallen empire. Few written records from the period remain. To understand the world of the Vikings, we must turn to archaeology.

BELOW
The ruins of the Benedictine monastery of Lindisfarne, Northumbria.

OPPOSITE
One of the 11th-century Viking ships on display at Roskilde Viking Museum in Denmark.

Raiders and Traders

Ragnar Hairy-breeks; Eric Bloodaxe; Ivar the Boneless; Eric the Red… the names read like a rogues' gallery, and with good reason. For while it may be true that the Vikings engaged in peaceful trading, loved a good story, worked metal brilliantly and were effective farmers, their record was also one of ruthless, murderous robbery.

Until recently, both archaeologists and historians agreed that the raid on the holy island of Lindisfarne (in the north of England) in 793 CE marked the beginning of the Viking era. However, two Viking ship burials accidentally discovered in the course of cable laying on the Estonian island of Saaremaa in 2008 are challenging this theory. University of Tartu archaeologist Marge Konsa led the dig

on the first boat, which held the remains of seven men aged between 18 and 45, together with their knives, whetstones and a bone comb. They had all died violently.

Radiocarbon dating of the boat timbers produced a surprising result: the vessel, which had no mast or sail, had been built between 650 and 700 – approximately 100 years before the Lindisfarne raid. The boat may have been used and repaired for decades prior to its final voyage.

Two years later, Jüri Peets from the University of Tallinn found a second, larger Viking ship nearby. As with the first, its timbers had rotted away; but the impression it had left in the soil and the position of the rivets and nails revealed that it was about 55 ft (17 m) long and 10 ft (3 m) wide. It had a keel, essential for seagoing, and Peets believes it also had a mast and a sail. If true, then *Salme 2* is the oldest sailing vessel ever found in the Baltic.

The dead men were buried in a significant way: five warriors with richly decorated, double-edged swords had been positioned at the top of the pile. The bodies with cruder, single-edged weapons lay at the bottom. The hierarchical order suggests a raiding party led by an élite. One of the leaders – perhaps a king – had a decorated walrus-ivory gaming piece in his mouth. There were also mutton and beef bones and the remains of dogs. Were these pets, or attack dogs? The bones of a goshawk and a sparrowhawk were also found, most likely used for hunting game along the coast.

Nobody knows whether these men were killed in an ill-fated raid on the island, or by rival Norse warriors. No matter how they died, the survivors buried them in haste. It is hoped isotope analysis can pinpoint their place of origin.

LEFT
A double-edge sword found amid the Viking-ship excavations in Estonia.

BITTER ENEMIES

Following the Lindisfarne raid, Viking raiding parties terrorized English shores, attacking villages along the coast and looting monasteries as they went. These were, however, just seasonal incursions – each winter they would return home to enjoy the spoils of the raiding season.

In 865 CE, this changed. A united coalition of Norse warriors, known as the "Great Heathen Army" by their Anglo-Saxon opponents, arrived on English shores intent on conquest. According to the Viking Sagas, the sons of Ragnar Lothbrok came on a mission of revenge, able to overcome their differences to subdue their English opponents. They would conquer the kingdoms of Northumbria, Mercia and East Anglia, with only Wessex avoiding their axe. Eventually, Alfred the Great stemmed the tide, defeating the Norsemen at Edington in 878 CE – but the respite was only temporary. Beginning in 1974, Martin Biddle and Birthe Kjølbye-Biddle excavated the site of St Wystan's Church at Repton, in Derbyshire. Referenced in the *Anglo-Saxon Chronicle*, the town was the winter base of the "Great Army" between 873 and 874 CE. They found a body buried with a piece of jewellery representing Thor's Hammer, with wounds on the skull and spine. Nearby, they found the remains of at least 250 more individuals, plus a central coffin containing what is believed to be the skeleton of the legendary Viking warrior, Ivar the Boneless. Mass graves found across the UK detail the conflict between Norseman and Anglo-Saxon. At Ridgeway, near Weymouth, a grave containing 54 skeletons, dating back to approximately 1000 CE, was discovered in 2009 (see image page 164). Isotope evidence showed the bodies were of Scandinavian origin – evidence of a Viking raiding party that came to a bloody end.

RIGHT
The statue of King Alfred the Great makes its presence felt in Winchester, capital of his kingdom of Wessex.

KING ARTHUR

Did King Arthur really exist? The legend of the Briton who led the defence against the Saxon invaders of the fifth and sixth centuries is compelling, but actual evidence for the tale popularized by the fanciful accounts of the medieval cleric Geoffrey of Monmouth is sparse. Brief mentions of the famous leader in the Venerable Bede's *Ecclesiastical History of the English People* and in the *Historia Brittonum* have added little to the factual database. According to legend, Tintagel in Cornwall was the birthplace of King Arthur. Pottery dating to the era was first discovered at the site by Raleigh Radford in the 1930s, but it has only been more recently that major archaeological investigations have been undertaken. In 1998, a stone inscribed with the name "Artognou" was discovered there and sparked speculation that the first evidence for the legendary leader was about to be uncovered. In 2016, the Cornwall Archaeological Unit, in association with English Heritage, unearthed the walls of a sixth-century palace. The team found more than 150 fragments from glass and pottery vessels, suggesting active international trade. Earthwork surveys showed evidence of 100 buildings. Whether this was truly the home of the legendary King Arthur or "merely" a royal palace of the Kingdom of Dumnonia, the excavations underway at Tintagel continue to reveal secrets about the so-called Dark Ages.

ABOVE
Tintagel, Cornwall, inextricably linked with King Arthur in folklore and myth. The clifftop castle outside the small town is thought to have been built about 1140 CE.

BELOW
The Artognou stone fuelled debate about Arthurian connections, but academics remain dubious as to its significance.

archaeologists in the past. That is now beginning to change.

Meanwhile, at Staraya Ladoga in western Russia, evidence of a 9th-century Viking settlement was uncovered in 1997, including Scandinavian jewellery and a burned-down Viking workshop. In nearby Dalnaja bay, a longship dating to the 10th century was also found. The largest Viking archaeological site in Russia is at Gnezdovo, located on the Dnieper River near Smolensk. Excavation of the site, which consists of 3,000 burial mounds, began in 1867, when a hoard of silver jewellery was first uncovered. Many of the items demonstrate a pronounced Viking presence, from jewellery to weaponry, but Byzantine and Arabic coins also show the importance of the site as

ABOVE
Viking graves found at Repton in Derbyshire revealed warriors alongside their tools and weapons, including this sword.

LEFT
Archaeologists today can study skeletons in minute detail, with injuries and other telling peculiarities teaching us much about life in times past.

BELOW
The Viking mass-grave excavation near Weymouth in Dorset.

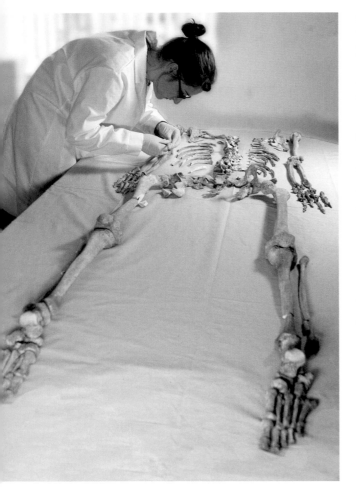

OVERSEAS ADVENTURES

The Vikings travelled far and wide from their Scandinavian homelands. Archaeologists have found extensive evidence of their presence in France, Italy, the Iberian peninsula and Russia. Dr Irene García Losquiño has investigated a number of anchors that washed up on a beach in Galicia. Nearby was a Viking-constructed mound called a *longphort* that closely resembled Viking camps in Ireland and England. The Vikings' presence in Iberia has received little attention from

The Sea Kings

With a commanding view of the River Deben, the open, estuary site of Sutton Hoo speaks of a high-living culture that used the sea as its Silk Road.

LEFT
Sifting earth around the Anglo-Saxon burial ship at Sutton Hoo in 1939.

RIGHT
The charismatic Sutton Hoo helmet, perhaps most striking of the many treasures unearthed at the site.

BELOW
A large gold belt buckle from the Sutton Hoo hoard, with intricate interlacing carved detail.

One summer night on the eve of World War II, Edith Pretty looked out of the window and saw a series of ghostly, warlike figures in armour walking across the fields outside. She rushed to the nearest museum in Ipswich, which recommended a local, self-taught archaeologist named Basil Brown to investigate the lozenge-shaped mounds around her property. Brown began work in 1938 and decided to tackle the largest, Mound 1. What he found changed British archaeology forever. Inside was the impressed shape of a buried longboat, and the grave goods of a great Saxon king, Raedwald. It was an entire ocean-going wooden vessel, 88 ft (27 m) long, rivets still in position.

When the Angles, Saxons, Jutes and Frisians invaded Britain, during the fifth and sixth centuries CE, the area conquered slowly became known as Angleland (England). Their several kingdoms, constantly at war with one another, sometimes acknowledged one of their rulers as the *Bretwalda*, or "High King". Straddling the margin between myth and history, Raedwald was one of these.

Within the ship was an extraordinary treasure trove which demonstrated that this culture had extraordinary levels of sophistication and artistic skill. It contained a sceptre; magnificent gold-and-garnet cloisonné jewellery including ornate garnet and gold shoulder clasps; a stock of domestic items for use in the next world; and a majestic, pattern-welded sword, its scabbard inlaid with intricate crosses and mushroom shapes. Crowning it all was a remarkable iron and bronze war helm and a huge boss shield. The helmet is one of only five known, and is extravagantly and delicately worked.

With cloaks from Syria, silver from Byzantium and bowls from Africa, the finds at Sutton Hoo proved that this was a thriving, commercially confident culture with a truly continental outlook.

an important part of an international trading system. The Slavs and Greeks described the Vikings as "Varangians", who sailed the river systems of Russia, raiding and trading just as they did elsewhere in Europe. Eventually, a group of these Norsemen settled in the region and formed the basis of Kievan Rus. It was through Russia that the Vikings made their way to Greece and the most spectacular city of medieval Europe, Constantinople. There, the names of two

Vikings are carved with runes on a marble balcony at Hagia Sophia (the former church and mosque, now a museum).

THE SPLENDOURS OF THE DARK AGES

Archaeological treasures abound in the world of the Dark Ages. From Anglo-Saxon hoards containing intricate jewellery and gleaming coins to

Viking settlements across the Atlantic, archaeological discoveries are revealing a world connected by trade, warfare and cultural exchange that makes the term "Dark Ages" an ugly misnomer. In a time of few written records, the material remains of these cultures has been incredibly revealing. Ongoing excavations at Tintagel, Galicia and Gnezdovo continue to uncover the Viking Age and distinguish myth from reality.

L'ANSE AUX MEADOWS

The 11th-century Viking settlement of L'Anse aux Meadows in Newfoundland, Canada, proves Norsemen discovered North America long before Christopher Columbus. Excavations of "Leif's Camp", named after Leif Erikson, who first made landfall there around 1000 CE, have revealed longhouses and workshops built in the same style and with the same methods as buildings from the same period in Greenland and Iceland, as well as evidence of contemporary Scandinavian iron working. Archaeologists are investigating a second possible Viking site at Port Rosée, 300 miles (483 km) south of L'Anse aux Meadows.

THE ARCHAEOLOGY OF THE AMERICAS

REWRITING THE HISTORY BOOKS

In North America, until the last five centuries, human history went unrecorded. With no written record, on this continent archaeology has been crucial to understanding the past. Pioneers such as Cyrus Thomas and Frederic Putnam slowly revealed the rich cultural identity hidden under the surface.

Who were the earliest Americans, and how and when did they get there? Until recently it was thought that there were no people on the continent at all before 14,000 years ago. New archaeological discoveries are now pushing back the clock. The Americas were the last great land mass to be colonized by humanity. How, why and when did people first arrive?

The planet was cold, and vast sheets of ice lay over most of North America, locking up so much of the world's water that sea levels were around 400 ft (120 m) lower than they are today. Vast stretches of ocean floor opened up and islands stopped being islands, and became peninsulas. People may have made their way south around 13,000 years ago, across the land bridge that once existed between Alaska and Russia. Much of this prehistoric valley – now known as "Beringia", after the Bering Straits – is underwater.

Above the Bluefish River in northern Yukon sit a series of limestone caves that have caused a stir in the archaeological community. In the 1970s, Jacques Cinq-Mars studied the many animal remains left in the caves for proof of human activity. New radiocarbon dating techniques now prove beyond reasonable doubt that humans lived in or visited the cave system at least 24,000 years ago, at the height of the last Ice Age. One horse jaw bone in particular shows evidence of distinct human cut marks.

Assuming the land bridge theory is correct, were the people who crossed it the same as the "Clovis People" whom archaeologists once thought were the first to inhabit the Americas? "Clovis Points" are beautifully carved stone arrowheads. Slender and fluted, they have been found all over North America, including the Beringia area. But there is a new twist in the tale: archaeologists are currently finding evidence at different dig sites – for example at Schaefer Farm, an hour north

RIGHT
Delicate but deadly: Clovis points.

BELOW
Mastodon molars: clear evidence of cut marks.

BOTTOM
Dr James Chatters, the first to realize the extreme age of "Kennewick Man".

of Chicago – that other groups, with older tool technologies were around well before the people who made the Clovis points. Their presence would suggest the Beringia theory is wrong.

A controversial 2017 study seeks to turn this thesis on its head. New radiocarbon results show a mastodon skeleton discovered by palaeontologists in San Diego in 1992 is 130,000 years old. It was discovered near a collection of stone tools – which had presumably been used to kill and skin it. from the Late Pleistocene period. The discovery is rewriting our understanding of the spread of the human species across the globe. If the clear cut marks plainly seen on its limbs were made by humans, then this implies that humans – or more precisely the predecessors of *Homo sapiens* – arrived in the Americas more than 100,000 years before anyone has previously believed.

As the Bering Sea hurls storms of new violence against the coast, the permafrost will erode away. This process of climate change could soon bring new revelations about the peopling of the Americas. The warmer temperatures are already revealing new layers of past history – for instance at the settlement of Nunalleq, the big melt is revealing evidence hidden in the ground for four-and-a-half centuries. The site shows that the Little Ice Age of the 1600s caused wars between different bands of Yupik. An entire settlement of 50

THE KENNEWICK MAN CONTROVERSY

In 1996, two students made a remarkable discovery in the Columbia River in Kennewick, Washington: a skeleton that was almost 9,000 years old. Will Thomas was getting ready to watch the town's annual boat race. He spotted what looked like a skull sticking out of the water. Thinking it was a boulder, Thomas decided to play a trick on his friend. He reached into the water and pulled the object free. It was indeed a human skull. Kennewick Man's skeleton was almost entirely intact, a rare occurrence. The discovery began a controversy that would last more than two decades. Local Native American tribes wanted the body of the man they described as "The Ancient One" returned to them under the Native American Graves Protection and Repatriation Act (NAGPRA). The archaeologist who had first carbon-dated Kennewick Man's skeleton, James Chatters, and the Smithsonian's forensic expert Douglas Owsley believed the bones were not genetically related to modern Native Americans. Physically, he resembled Polynesian peoples more. The court case lasted nine years. More than a decade after its discovery, on 18 February 2017, a coalition of Columbia Basin tribes reburied the body.

people appears to have been smoked out of their sod hut and slaughtered, probably for their food.

A Forgotten World

Impressive sites like Serpent Mound, Chaco Canyon and the Verde Valley show that Native American civilizations were far more complex than their European colonizers first believed.

In the wild 1860s, the first groups of miners, soldiers and explorers arrived in central Arizona's Verde Valley. About 100 ft (34 m) above Beaver Creek, they found a dramatic 20-room, multi-storey dwelling built up into a sheer limestone cliff. It was obvious that the structure had been abandoned for a very long time, and the stone floors were covered with bat lime.

The newcomers dubbed the structure "Montezuma's Castle", reasoning that such building skills must have been Aztec, not Native American. The "Castle" was built by the Sinagua people, close relatives of the Hohokam people who dominated the ancient Southwest.

Archaeological evidence suggests a sequence of settlements, beginning around 900 CE, was interrupted by a volcanic eruption. Despite its sophistication, by 1425, the Verde Valley site had been abandoned: but no one knows quite why.

It is so high up that its inhabitants must have used rope ladders to make their precarious way into their homes. In the 1870s, Colonel Hiram C. Hodge only managed to reach it by "clinging to poles and jutting points of rock".

It is estimated that some 50 people could have lived here at a time. Archaeological discoveries in the lower section of the valley show the "castle" type of structure was the exception, not the rule: by 1300, most of the estimated 6–8,000 people then present in the area were living in small villages on the valley bottom. A large amount of what we do know about the people comes from the less spectacular

ABOVE
Man in the High Castle: the so-called "Montezuma Castle".

OPPOSITE ABOVE
The Sinagua occupied a large part of Arizona. Petroglyphs of water birds show their preoccupation with nature.

OPPOSITE BELOW
Monk's Mound, named for Trappist monks who set up home beneath it, drawn by William McAdams in 1887

"Castle A" nearby, which was spared the large-scale looting from which the more picturesque "Montezuma" suffered.

In 1906, President Theodore Roosevelt proclaimed "Montezuma Castle" a national monument. This was the first prehistoric ruin in the US to be protected under the 1906 Antiquities Act. The looting had finally been stopped.

MOUND BUILDERS

The sophisticated city of Cahokia was a medieval Manhattan, peopled by many First Nation tribes. By 1050, this Mississippian metropolis was a major centre of some 30,000 people; yet, by 1350, it had been abandoned. Why?

THE FATHER OF AMERICAN ARCHAEOLOGY

Frederic Putnam (1839–1915) was the archaeologist responsible for developing two of the most respected anthropological departments in the United States – at Harvard University and the University of California, Berkeley. He also developed the Peabody Museum, the American Museum of Natural History, Chicago's Field Museum of Natural History and Berkeley's Anthropological Museum. He was active in the field, too. He made several excavations at Serpent Mound in Southern Ohio between 1880 and 1895. Putnam dedicated much of his life to saving a place that inspired him "with a singular sensation of awe". Encouraging private donations from "a group of Boston ladies", he and the historian Francis Parkman bought the site and turned it into a public park. In 1991, a team of archaeologists reopened one of Putnam's original trenches, finding bits of charcoal that are now possible to date via Carbon-14 dating. Tests indicated the mound's most likely builders were the "Fort Ancient" villagers from c. 10–15,000 BCE.

"THE SERPENT,"
(Estey 1914)
ADAMS COUNTY OHIO.
E. G. Squier & E. H. Davis Surveyor 1846.

The city was 9 square miles (23.3 sq km) with 120 earthen mounds inside its borders, and appears to have been a spiritual magnet, drawing people from afar. The largest structure, known as Monk's Mound, was a colossus made up of more than 22 million cubic ft (623,000 cubic m) of soil. It must have taken the labour of thousands, as the lawyer Henry Brackenridge wrote to his friend Thomas Jefferson.

The city lay at the centre of a nationwide trading network that stretched as far as the Great Lakes and the Gulf coast. Its inhabitants lived well-fed lives and cultivated goosefoot and amaranth, as well as corn. They also smelted copper. Cahokia's 2-mile- (3.2-km) long

ABOVE LEFT
Frederic Ward Putnam.

LEFT
From Ancient Monuments to the Mississippi, a landmark publication by journalist Ephraim Squier and Dr Edwin Davis in 1848.

BELOW
An effigy pipe made from flint clay found at the Spiro Mounds site in Oklahoma.

palisade was surrounded by hundreds of thatched homes with wooden post walls. The people linked their quarters with courtyards, plazas, pathways and roads and lived cheek by jowl with a constant stream of incomers. Strontium tests on teeth have found that at least a third of the population was from elsewhere in America.

Twentieth-century development took a terrible toll on Cahokia, with one mound entirely destroyed by farming, and the place being used variously as a gamblin hall and even a pornographic drive-in. President Dwight Eisenhower's interstate highway programme finally paid the bill for archaeologosts to investigate sites in its path, and put Cahokia on the map.

A university team from Wisconsin-Milwaukee began mapping the site in 1966. They soon discovered that Cahokia had been built very suddenly in what they now call a "Big Bang". Yet the mysterious abandonment question has still not been answered. Tim Pauketat at the University of Illinois believes that Cahokia controlled outlying villages and that they supplied tributes to élites within the city.

The discovery of one mound with sinister mass burials, most of young women, suggests that ritual human sacrifice may have been practised.

ABOVE
Archaeologists excavate a rubbish dump, part of Monk's Mound in Cahokia Mounds State Park in 1972.

Historic Jamestowne

The story of the "lost fort" at America's first European settlement had fascinated American archaeologists for decades, but its location continued to elude them. An excavation by the National Park Service had turned up nothing. Dr William Kelso believed they were looking in the wrong place. Convinced that the 17th-century brick church tower was a part of the original fort, he soon found evidence of pottery fragments and weapons in the area, hinting that his educated guess was correct.

POCAHONTAS

You might think that Pocahontas was a legend – but not only did she exist, hers is also a genuine tale of crossing cultures. A member of the indigenous Powhatan tribe, the real Pocahontas brought food to the first, starving settlers of Jamestown; and by marrying one of them, John Rolfe, she also effected an uneasy peace. When she was 21, Pocahontas visited England where she met King James II – and contracted the tuberculosis that killed her.

In 1994, the Jamestown Rediscovery Project was launched after extensive preliminary work and negotiations with Preervation Virginia. More than 20 years later, the team has located not just the fort and the original settlement, but the remains of some of the founders themselves – along with artefacts that speak volumes about their lives.

By 2010, they had located the site of the first church. There, they discovered the graves of the founders of the first permanent British settlement in America. Excavators uncovered a body buried with a captain's staff, which was only carried by British officers, suggesting it was Captain Gabriel Archer. High-resolution CT scans revealed the silver box found resting on the coffin was a Catholic reliquary, complete with a crucifix and holy oils. This in itself was a revelation, as Archer had ostensibly been leading a band of devout Protestants. The other bodies were identified through multiple lines of evidence, including chemical analyses, 3D imaging and their teeth. They were the Rev. Robert Hunt; Sir Ferdinando Wainman and Captain William West.

Those who had been in the New World the longest had extensive tooth decay and abscesses: corn leaves a sugary residue, which is much worse for your teeth than the barley and wheat-based diet of Europe. Nevertheless, they would have been grateful for that corn: during the "starving time" – a six-month period following their arrival – 250 people perished.

Ultimately, Jamestown only survived with the help of Powhatan, chief of the Powhatan Indians of Tidewater. Another long-term excavation project in Virginia, of a Monacan village, is revealing a more complex picture. Project leader Jeffrey Hantman of the University of Virginia

Ancient church Jamestown - 1864.

ABOVE
A drawing made in
1864 of the church at
Jamestown.

RIGHT
Dr William Kelso on
site at the Jamestown
Redicovery Project.

wants to examine why Powhatan opted
to side with the settlers. Artefacts which
Hantman has found so far suggest that
Powhatan was dependent for his wealth
on trading copper. In trading his corn for
John Smith's copper, he gained the upper
hand on his Monacan rivals.

Today, "Historic Jamestowne" is
a beacon example of a visit-friendly
excavation. It is well worth exploring its
website; you can watch the digging or
even book a tour with the Director of
Archaeology, Dr William Kelso.

CULTURAL GIANTS

In Mesoamerica and South America, civilizations flourished before the arrival of Columbus. When the Spanish invaders arrived, they found cities larger than anything they had seen in Europe, beautiful architecture, complex social structures and elaborate religious rituals. The conquest of the Aztec and Inca empires and the subsequent desire to consolidate Spanish rule meant that the authorities sought to suppress these cultures. The great civilizations of the Americas faded into the background until adventurous travellers and amateur archaeologists began to uncover the extensive history that lay beneath their feet.

In spite of one hundred years of research, archaeologists have only scratched the surface of the history buried under the huge landmass of South America. New technology is beginning to re-write the history of its early cultures, in particular the million-dollar LiDAR scanners that can probe laser light through remote jungle from the air.

From 1200 BCE onwards, the precocious Olmec culture created Mesoamerica's first great art style on Mexico's Gulf Coast, with its mysterious monumental, 9-ft (3-m)-high, sculpted heads of rulers. Soon the complex Mayan city-states arose further south, whose stone reliefs mark key events in the lives of their kings and queens. On Peru's Pacific north coast, Caral may have been the first urban complex in the Americas.

In highland Mexico, by 600 CE, Teotihuacan housed as many as 200,000 inhabitants, one of the six largest urban centres of its time. It was one of the first sites to be excavated in the Americas. During the late 17th century, Carlos de Siguenza y Góngora, a creole priest and poet born in New Spain, dug around the Pyramid of the Sun at Teotihuacan. He advanced the theory that the indigenous Mexicans were actually descendants of Egyptians.

Serious archaeological investigation of Teotihuacan began in the early 20th century with the work of Porfirio Díaz Leopoldo Batres. The magnificent ziggurats of the city were the earliest examples of public architecture, attempts to control the invisible forces of nature that govern the success or failure of crops. There are no towers or defences at abandoned Teotihuacan, the model metropolis, but we do know that sacrifice, both animal and human, took place in front of thousands of spectators. Sacred sites and temples such as the kalasasaya (sacred enclosure) at Tiwanaku and the Templo Mayor (great temple) at Tenochtitlan are meticulously planned around key sunrises and sunsets in the calendar.

EMPIRES OF THE AMERICAS - ANDES

3500–1800 BCE	100 BCE–800 CE	100–800	300–1150	500–1000	900–1476	1476–1534
Norte Chico	Nazca	Moche	Tiwanaku	Wari	Chimu	Inca

Ruins Beneath the Roads

The Aztec empire developed extensive trade networks in symbolically powerful materials such as the shimmering, iridescent feathers of the quetzal bird. It promoted a militaristic state ideology.

Beneath the busy roads of Mexico City lies the ancient city of Tenochtitlan. For years, the Aztec capital languished forgotten beneath the modern capital. Then. in 1978, electrical workers laying cables accidentally came across the Aztec Templo Mayor. They found a monolith with a relief of Coyolxauhqui. Eduardo Matos Moctezuma directed

Empires of the Americas - Mexico

1200–400 BCE	***c.*1–650** CE	**400** BCE**–1521** CE	**900–1168**	**1428–1521**
Olmec	Teotihuacan	Zapotec	Toltec	Mexica (Aztec)

THE COLLAPSE OF THE MAYA

Sophisticated civilization took longer to take root in the Maya lowlands than in the Mexican highlands. The environment was not a natural "cradle of civilization". Dense jungle, limited rainfall and dangerous wildlife made the establishment of empires in the region more difficult. Yet, by the middle of the 1st millennium CE, the Maya were the predominant power in Mesoamerica.

Excavations of the site of Cuello in northern Belize by Norman Hammond provide a fascinating insight into the emergence of this civilization. Maize husks discovered at the site have shown how the staple crop was responsible for an population explosion of the Maya population. Both the size of the maize cob and the yields of maize steadily increased between 1000 BCE and 200 CE. Hammond also discovered pieces of jade in graves, hinting that an élite was in place well before the Classic Maya period.

Great cities developed in the tropical jungles of the Yucatan. Beautiful sculpture, intricate artwork and spectacular pyramids displayed the influence of Mayan civilization for all to see. The Mayan command of mathematics and astronomy was extraordinarily advanced. Their hieroglyphic system of writing was as complex as it was intriguing. The exploration of Mayan civilization began with two Victorians, one American and one English:

John Lloyd Stephens and Frederick Catherwood. Stephens was an explorer, writer and occasional politician, while Catherwood was an artist and engineer. They had both read intriguing accounts of lost cities hidden in the Mesoamerican jungle and set out to find them. In 1834, they arrived at Copán and soon moved on to chart the other great Mayan cities – Palenque, Uxmal and Chichen Itza. When they returned to New York in June 1842, they jointly published *Incidents of*

THE MAYA

1800 BCE–250 CE	250–900	500–600	750
Preclassic Maya	Classic Maya	The Rise of Tikal	Conflicts arise between Mayan city states and trading partners

Travel in Yucatán, an illustrated account of the Mayan civilization that pioneered the study of the Maya as a serious archaeological subject.

At the end of the 9th century CE, Mayan society collapsed with shocking suddenness. Inscriptions on monuments, tomb temples and royal funerary cults disappeared almost overnight. The great cities were abandoned and no new ones rose to replace them.

How did such a formidable civilization disappear so completely?

In the past, both historians and archaeologists pointed to factors such as civil war, invasion and the collapse of trade routes as the culprits. But today, most experts are looking to another explanation: man-made changes to the environment. Drought seems to have been a factor in the Mayan civilization's long decline. Population growth had spurred intense agricultural cultivation of maize in the region. This caused deforestation and the degradation of the soil, making the region simultaneously more vulnerable to flooding and drought. Far from being passive subjects of their environment, the Maya, like indigenous peoples across the Americas, had shaped the ecology they lived and worked within. In the 9th century, their impact on the environment caught up with them, and the record shows that the region suffered its worst drought for thousands of years.

The evidence has been growing. Douglas Kennett, heading a team of archaeologists, analysed thousands of samples of a 2,000-year-old stalagmite

LEFT
Symbolically decorated, this censer would have been used to hold a bowl for burning incense.

BELOW
John Lloyd Stephens. As well as his archaeological work, Stephens was also involved in the planning of the Panama railway.

750–900	899	900–1500	900–1050	1224
Chichen Itza develops	Tikal is abandoned	Postclassic Maya	Chichen Itza becomes a regional power	Chichen Itza is abandoned

at Yok Balum cave in Belize to confirm the theory in 2012. In total, nine different institutions were involved in the project. Scientists from Rice University and Louisiana State University studied sediment samples from Belize's Great Blue Hole, a 400-ft (122-m)-deep cave in a barrier reef. Layers from the era of the Mayan decline between 800 and 1000 CE. The presence of high levels of aluminium and titanium suggested to the researchers that heavy rainfall from intense tropical cyclones was pounding material out of the rock and into the sea.

While the great cities of the south, such as Tikal and Palenque, were abandoned, in modern day Guatemala and Belize, the cities of the north continued to survive and even thrive, including the most famous of all Mayan cities, Chichen Itza.

An extended drought beginning in 1020 CE triggered political insecurity and increased warfare. This was followed by disastrous population collapse, perhaps the result of very sudden climate change. Even a minor drought could lead to the collapse of a carefully balanced ecosystem. By the time the Spanish conquistadors arrived in the 16th century, the great Mayan civilization was already fading into the jungle.

WILLIAM GADOURY

It took a tech-savvy, 15-year-old Canadian, William Gadoury, to locate a "missing" Mayan city hidden deep in the Yucatan peninsula. Gadoury proposed that the Mayan cities scattered through Mexico, Honduras, Guatemala and El Salvador lined up exactly with major stellar constellations. Yet one city appeared to be missing. The teenager persuaded scientists at the Canadian Space Agency to focus its satellite imaging equipment on a significant spot where a star remained unmatched. Using Google Earth, he named the missing city K'aak Chi, or Mouth of Fire. Imagery of the site clearly showed a square, man-made formation concealed beneath the dense forest. The story attracted international attention, but some cast doubt on Gadoury's theory. Many archaeologists question if the Maya could have had the knowledge to arrange their cities in this higly symbolic way. Gadoury's extremely remote "lost" city remains as yet unexplored.

THE LORD OF SIPÁN

South America's cultural patrimony has been plundered for hundreds of years. Peruvian archaeologist Walter Alva saved the spectacular tomb of the Lord of Sipán from a similar fate. In 1987, the director of the National Archaeological Museum received a call in the middle of the night. Tomb-robbers had found the grave of a high-ranking Mohican warrior-priest and taken precious gold and silver treasure. Within hours, it would be headed for the black market – and out of the country. When he first arrived on the scene, the impoverished local community had descended upon the Huaca Rajada, consisting of two adobe pyramids and a low platform, in the hopes of finding valuable leftovers. With the help of the police, government funds and National Geographic, Alva and his team were able persuade them to stop the looting. There, they uncovered the elaborate tomb of the Lord of Sipán, a Mochican lord, and six other people. A total of 451 ceremonial items were discovered at the site. Excavations continued, and two more tombs were found.

and routes. The most impressive Inca archaeological site is at Machu Picchu (see pages 54–7). The Incas captured the sacred objects of their enemies and symbolically imprisoned them in their Coricancha temple/fortress at Cuzco that was dedicated to Quilla, the goddess of the moon. The temple was covered in silver, thought to be the tears of moonlight. Coricancha, or The Golden Enclosure, was the centre of the Inca world. In the great temple of Inti, the golden walls were studded with emeralds. Their star religious icon, the golden statue of Inti, was taken to a place of safety when the Spanish arrived, but has never been found again.

A WORLD TO BE DISCOVERED

Despite extensive efforts by archaeologists in Central and South America, the surface has only begun to be scratched. New cities remain to be discovered in the Honduran rainforest. Secrets remain hidden underneath the roads of Mexico City. And in the Andes, thousands of projects to uncover the legacy of the Inca and their predecessors continue. The challenges of looting remain. For archaeologists to be successful, academics and governments alike will have to remain vigilant against those who seek to plunder ancient tombs for wealth or fame.

ABOVE
A reconstruction of the tomb of the Lord of Sipán at Huaca Rajada.

RIGHT
A cult figurine from the Inca period.

LEFT
The terraces and Temple Hill of Ollantaytambo in Peru that were the royal palace of the Incan emperor, Pachacuti.

ABOVE
Beautifully detailed, this is one of a pair of earflares made
by the Moche. Earflares were large, circular adornments,
popular among Peruvian lords as a sign of status and
wealth.

Dedicated to Inti, the temple of Coricancha was once the most important in the Incan empire. Its walls were originally covered in gold and it was fabulously decorated throughout. Spanish colonists demolished the temple and used the foundations to build the Church of Santo Domingo.

ABOVE
Beautifully detailed, this is one of a pair of earflares made by the Moche. Earflares were large, circular adornments, popular among Peruvian lords as a sign of status and wealth.

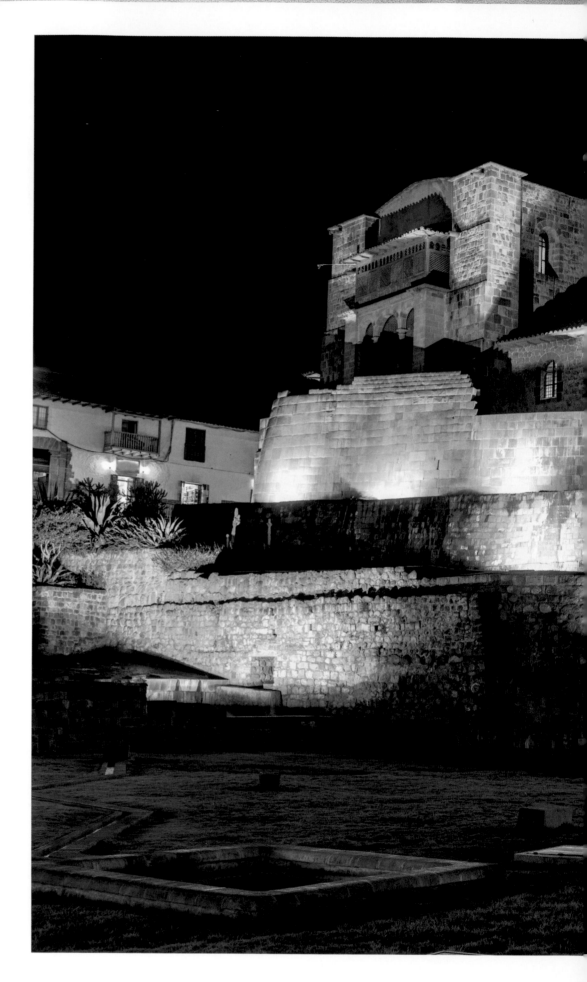

RIGHT
Dedicated to Inti, the temple of Coricancha was once the most important in the Incan empire. Its walls were originally covered in gold and it was fabulously decorated throughout. Spanish colonists demolished the temple and used the foundations to build the Church of Santo Domingo.

THE ARCHAEOLOGY OF ASIA

FROM THE QIN TO THE MING

The epic sweep of Chinese history between the coronation of the first Qin emperor, Qin Shi Huang (also known as Shi Huangdi), in 221 BCE and the fall of the Ming dynasty in 1644 CE saw a pattern of unification under an immensely powerful dynasty, followed by years of violent internal conflict.

A UNIQUE LEGACY

Archaeology has been practised in China since as long ago as the Song dynasty (960–1279 CE), when local gentry, scholars and bureaucrats recovered artefacts dating back to the Shang dynasty. Like the European antiquarians (see pages 19–24), their main interest was in acquiring ancient objects for their own personal pleasure rather than analysis of past cultures. Many hoped to use the artefacts they found for state rituals. The scholar Shen Kuo (1031–1095 CE) in his *Dream Pool Essays* castigated his contemporaries' superficial approach to archaeology and emphasized the importance of studying the original purpose and construction of ancient items.

Shen Kuo's warnings did not go entirely unheeded. Ouyang Xiu (1007–1072 CE) created 400 rubbings of inscriptions found on bronze and stone relics,

PREVIOUS PAGES
Charismatic carvings on the long-hidden Angkor Wat complex in Cambodia.

ABOVE
A Chinese bronze ritual wine container from the late Shang dynasty, dated to the 11th century BCE.

LEFT
As well as his interest in archaeology, Song-dynasty scientist and astronomer Shen Kuo designed astronomical instruments and a solar calendar.

DYNASTIES OF CHINA

221 BCE–206 BCE	206 BCE–220 CE	220–280	265–420	420–589	581–618
Qin	Han	Three Kingdoms	Jin	Northern and Southern dynasties	Sui

THE GREAT WALL OF CHINA

No single structure better encapsulates the reach, ambition and potency of China than the Great Wall. For the Chinese, it marked the point where civilization ended. A survey in 2012, using GPS and infrared to chart the course of the wall, concluded that its maximum length was a startling 13,247 miles (21,196 km). The emperor Qin Shi Huang began the construction of the "Long Wall of 10,000 Li" in the late 3rd century BCE to provide a defensive barrier against the nomadic Xiongnu people to the north. During the Han dynasty, it was needed to protect the increasingly vital trade routes of the Silk Road. By the 6th century, as many 1.8 million men at a time were required to repair and reinforce the wall, and it would be repeatedly rebuilt over at least 1,700 years. It is hardly surprising, therefore, that many stretches of the wall remaining today, which are mostly the work of the Ming, look quite different from the original construction.

ABOVE
A section of the Great Wall at Jinshanling, close to Beijing and accessible today. More remote sections are much wilder – equally impressive but with a different ambience.

LEFT
Johan Gunnar Andersson, the Swedish archaeologist/geologist, photographed in China in 1920.

while Lü Dalin (1046–92 CE) made the practice of archaeology more systematic, creating the *Koagutu*, or *Illustrated Catalogue of Examined Antiquity*, in 1092 which detailed the ancient objects that had been discovered. A formal system of dating soon followed, classifying objects according to their inscriptions, shapes and motifs.

Modern scientific Chinese archaeology began with the Swedish archaeologist Johan Gunnar Andersson (1874–1960). He arrived in China as a mining consultant. Working with Chinese colleagues such as Yuan Fuli, he found prehistoric remains in Henan Province along the Yellow River. In his role in China's National Geological Survey, he helped train a generation of Chinese archaeologists.

HONOURING THE DEAD

Emperor Qin Shi Huang's achievements were astonishing – he united the warring kingdoms of China into a single empire, built the Great Wall and established China's legal and political system for years to come.

618–907	907–960	960–1279	1271–1368	1368–1644
Tang	Five Dynasties and Ten Kingdoms	Song, Liao, Jin and Western Xia	Yuan	Ming

BELOW
One of the extraordinary, characterful terracotta warriors from the Qin emperor's vast army, ready to serve in the imperial afterlife.

His final resting place was as magnificent as his reign. In 1974, farmers digging a well near the city of Xi'an stumbled across one of the greatest archaeological finds of Chinese history: the mausoleum of the first emperor. Among other surprises, the huge tomb complex revealed a pristine army of thousands of terracotta warriors guarding their emperor (see pages 70–3). The government dispatched a team of archaeologists to learn more. As many as 8,000 figures have been found in the tomb, along with horse-drawn chariots and weapons. Much of the subterranean complex remains unexcavated. Today, Chinese archaeologists using remote sensors have found another underground chamber, filled with figures posed as dancers, musicians and acrobats, but excavations have been temporarily halted for fear of damaging the site.

The most impressive of China's many other royal tombs – at least of those found so far – is at Mawangdui in Changsha in the centre of the country, where three second-century BCE tombs were excavated between 1972 and 1974. When archaeologists opened up Tomb No. 1, that of Xin Zhui, the wife of the Marquis of Dai, they found it perfectly preserved. A wealth of artefacts were interred with her, including 152 "tomb figures" representing dancers, musicians and servants. There were everyday items, such as a tray with bowls and cups and a pair of chopsticks. Xin Zhui also took to her grave various cosmetic boxes, vases, arm rests and screens. On one side of the tomb were bamboo cases containing herbal medicines, silk garments and other clothes. Draped on the coffin was a spectacular T-shaped red silk banner representing her journey to the afterworld. Painted at the top is a vision of heaven, protected by two guards; below is an image of Xin Zhui flanked by two servants; and at the bottom are scenes from the underworld.

These impressive tombs required the work of thousands of labourers and provide compelling evidence of the wealth and reach of Han-dynasty China. Such marvellous burial procedures would not be seen again until the Ming dynasty.

LAND OF THE THREE WAYS

By 500 BCE, Buddhism had spread rapidly across China. A series of sites discovered towards the end of the 19th century attest to the enduring vibrancy of the religion. At Dazu in Sichuan province, an exceptional series of religious figures were carved into the rockface.

Perhaps the single most remarkable site, however, is the warren of tunnels – the Caves of the Thousand Buddhas, or Mogao Caves – near the Silk Road settlement of Dunhuang in northwest China. They contain 487 lavishly decorated cave-temples, dug between 366 CE and 1368, and covering an area of 490,000 sq ft (44,500 sq m). The first caves were discovered in 1900 by a Daoist monk, Wang Yuanlu. In

LEFT
The red silk banner from Mawangdui's Tomb No. 1, dating from the Western Han period. A glorious, dragon-filled progression between heaven and hell, its purpose was to help the spirit ascend heavenwards.

BELOW
The "Three Worthies of Huayan" (Manjushri, Vairocana and Samantabhadra), Buddhist deity carvings at Baodingshan, near Dazu in Sichuan province.

the following years they were extensively investigated by teams from Britain, France, Japan and Russia.

In addition to 2,400 clay sculptures and 1,100 scrolls, 15,000 books printed on paper were found in what is known as the Library Cave. They were apparently hidden here for safe-keeping in approximately 1000 CE. Among the scrolls is a copy of the *Diamond Sutra*. Dating from 868 CE, it is the world's oldest complete printed document.

Maritime Traders

In recent times, archaeologists all over the world have increasingly used new technology to delve beneath the waves (see page 246). China is no exception. In 1987, the Underwater Archaeology Research Center was set up as a division of the National Museum of China.

IMPERIAL FAREWELLS

If the Forbidden City in Beijing, begun in 1420, remains the most opulent expression of the lavish, highly ceremonial world of the Ming, the 13 Ming tombs, covering 15 square miles (40 sq km) at Changping, 26 miles (42 km) north of Beijing, are the dynasty's most compelling archaeological record. The remains of the Ming rulers from the Yongle emperor to the Chongzhen emperor lie in a series of mausoleums, the first constructed in 1409 and a final one completed on the death of the Ming emperor in 1644. Access to the tombs is via the "Sacred Way", an avenue lined with statues of lions, elephants, camels and bodyguards.

OPPOSITE TOP
The statue-lined Sacred Way to the Ming tombs.

BELOW
A panoramic view of the Ming tombs, painted during the 18th century.

Only one of the 13 tombs has so far been excavated. This is Dingling, the tomb of Zhu Yijun (1572–1620), the terrifyingly corpulent Wanli emperor whose legendary indolence goes some way towards explaining the eventual collapse of Ming rule. It is the third-largest of the Ming tombs. Built 89 ft (27 m) below ground, it had survived the centuries intact, safe from the depradations of looters and grave-robbers who have plagued so many archaeological sites. Following pleas from the archaeologists Guo Moruo and

Wu Han in 1956, the site was hurriedly excavated on government orders. An astonishingly imposing complex, comprising five separate stone chambers behind two sets of immense self-locking marble doors, came to light. The fifth and final chamber was the tomb of the emperor and his two wives. Porcelain vases containing oil and a wick had been left to light the mausoleum for eternity.

The challenges faced by the Dingling excavation persuaded the Chinese government to suspend further excavation except for rescue purposes. The remaining Ming Tombs are still unopened.

BELOW
This hand-sized piece of gold jewellery, with ruby, pearl and other gemstones, echoes the shape of the Chinese character meaning "heart". It is from Dingling.

BOTTOM
The Changling Ming tomb. The largest and best preserved of the 13, it houses the mausoleum of the third Ming sovereign, called Zhu Di or the Yongle emperor, and his empress, Xu.

Its researchers have made impressive discoveries that are rewriting the history of China's maritime and trading past. Archaeologists are also unearthing evidence of an equally prosperous "Maritime Silk Road". In that same year, a team of British and Chinese archaeologists searching for an East India Company wreck instead found a 98-ft (30-m) 800-year-old Chinese shipwreck in the South China Sea. Nanhai No. 1 was dated to between 1127 and 1279 CE.

An extensive rescue operation began in 2007. Surveys of the wreck revealed that it contained more than 60,000 items. Following its transfer to the Maritime Silk Road Museum in Guangdong, excavation of the wreckage continued under the gaze of crowds of inquisitive tourists. The ship held porcelain and ceramics for trade, vast numbers of copper coins and personal items, including gold jewellery, which suggested that a number of wealthy merchants and passengers were on board when it sank. The vessel's importance as an archaeological find is rivalled only by the Terracotta Army.

ALL UNDER HEAVEN

Modern China has spent billions creating a pool of well-trained state archaeologists, rebuilding its cultural identity after the Cultural Revolution. It is now even venturing outside its own borders, for example, with a dig in India at a Bronze Age site in Rakhigarhi, north of Delhi.

OPPOSITE
The frontispiece of the oldest known printed book in the world, a Chinese edition of the *Diamond Sutra*, found in the Mogao Caves in Dunhaung.

BELOW
A ceramic bowl featuring a flower design, salvaged from Nanhai No. 1 shipwreck and now in Guangdong Art Museum.

The Land of the Rising Sun

"The Ancestors" are very important in the spiritual life of Japan, and the Japanese have a long history of archaeological enquiry. The historian Lord Tokugawa Mitsukuni was eager to re-establish loyalty to the Japanese emperor. As early as 1692, he began Japan's first scientific excavation of an imperial tomb in Ohtawara City. It dated from the Kofun period (300–700 CE), Japan's early prehistoric era. These keyhole-shaped mounds (*kofun*) are unique to Japan.

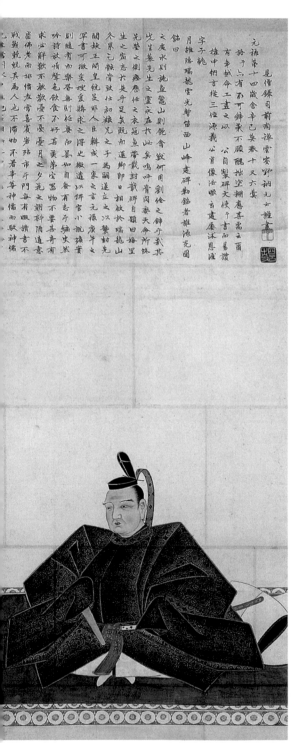

The story of Japanese archaeology as a systematic discipline really began in 1877 when the American zoologist and orientalist Edward Sylvester Morse excavated the Omori Shell Mounds. Morse and his team discovered a style of pottery there that they described as "cord-marked". In Japanese, this translates as Jōmon, which became the term used for the early period of Japanese history (c. 14,000–1000 BCE), when this style of pottery was produced.

Competing theories

During the late 19th and early 20th centuries, Japanese scholars debated the origins of the Japanese people. Some believed they descended from a people called the Yayoi, who flourished from 300 BCE to 300 CE. Others believed the ancestors of the Japanese were the Ainu, the indigenous people of Hokkaido (Japan's second largest island). Still others claimed the Japanese had the same ethnic origin as the Ryukyuan people, indigenous people of the Ryukyu Islands. An early aim of Japanese archaeologists was to test these theories. There were often racist undertones to these debates, as many scholars regarded the Ainu as "primitive", and were keen to disprove any ancestral connection between them and the "civilized" modern Japanese.

ABOVE
Beautifully carved, this wooden Netsuke figure depicts an elderly Ainu man.

LEFT
Tokugawa Mitsukuni, under whose authority the Mitogaku scholars put together a major history of Japan.

Western techniques

In 1916, Japan's first university archaeology department was established at Kyoto Imperial University. The department's first professor, Kosaku Hamada, had spent time studying in Britain, and he introduced Western archaeological methods and theories to Japan on his return. In 1922, he published Japan's first ever archaeology textbook, *Tsuron Kokogaku* (*An Introduction to Archaeology*), which is still in print today.

ARCHAEOLOGICAL PERIODS IN JAPAN

14,000–1,000 BCE	1,000 BCE–300 CE	250–530	530–710	710–794	794–1185
Jōmon	Yayoi	Kofun - Yamato	Asuka - Yamato	Nara	Heian

LEFT
A fine example of Jōmon earthenware with its distinctive corded decoration and incised patterns.

RIGHT
Sweden commemorates Oscar Montelius on a postage stamp.

BELOW
A shell mound in Okinawa being excavated by the archaeologists Iha Fuyu (left) and Torii Ryuzo (right).

Hamada introduced the concept of seriation as a relative dating method for Japanese pottery. Seriation, developed by the Swedish archaeologist Oscar Montelius, looks at factors like design style and the quantity of objects sharing a particular style, as a way of establishing the chronology of an object. Through the use of this technique, Sugao Yamanouchi at the University of Tokyo was able to demonstrate that the Jōmon was a hunter-gatherer society, whereas the Yayoi was an agricultural one.

Using another Western technique, stratigraphy, Kosaku Hamada overturned myths about the prehistoric origins of the Japanese. In 1917, Hamada excavated at Kou, Osaka Prefecture, and in 1918–19, he excavated at Ibusuki, Kagoshima Prefecture. Here, the stratigraphy revealed that the Jōmon and Yayoi cultures came from different layers. Until this time, the two cultures were regarded as separate but contemporaneous. Hamada conclusively showed that the Jōmon culture predated the Yayoi.

SHELL MOUNDS

Edward Morse's excavation at Omori, Japan, in 1877 was one of the world's first archaeological excavations of a shell mound. These are human-made mounds where the debris from cooking and eating shellfish have accumulated over time. They are useful to archaeologists as a record of people's diet, and also because they contain fragments of stone tools and household goods. Because shells are rich in calcium carbonate, shell mounds tend to be alkaline, which slows the normal rate of decay caused by soil acidity. This means that organic material, including food, clothing and human remains, often survives in shell mounds for archaeologists to study.

THE JAPANESE ARCHAEOLOGICAL ASSOCIATION

The post-war period witnessed a major expansion of Japanese archaeology. The founding of the Japanese Archaeological Association (JAA) in 1948 led to an increase in collaboration among archaeologists from all over Japan.

The inspiration for the JAA was an excavation at Toro, an archaeological site in Suruga Ward, Shizuoka City, dated to the 1st century CE, which began in 1947. Discovered in 1943, Toro was the first archaeological site found to contain Yayoi-era wet-rice paddy fields. Also excavated at the site were pit-dwellings, refuse pits, raised-floor buildings and even the well-preserved remains of wooden farm tools. The excavation generated considerable interest from newspapers and radio stations, raising public awareness of Japan's ancient history.

The Toro excavation ended in 1950. Over the following eight years the JAA organized excavations at 21 other Yayoi-era sites, from Kyushu in the west to Aichi Prefecture in central Japan.

The JAA also played a major role in formulating rules governing archaeological excavations and the preservation of historic sites. This first became an issue following a fire that broke out in the great hall of Hōryūji, an ancient Buddhist temple in Nara, on 26 January 1949. Hōryūji dates from the 7th or 8th century and is one of the oldest wooden buildings in the world. The accident, which resulted in the destruction of several beautiful murals, prompted the Japanese national legislature to pass the Law of Protection of Cultural Properties (1950). The law, which the JAA helped to draft, codified the rules relating to archaeological excavations. Prior to 1950, anyone could excavate archaeological sites. From this point on, archaeologists had to obtain formal permission for an excavation from the national government.

DISASTER-LED ARCHAEOLOGY

Japan is one of the most earthquake-prone nations in the world, and this poses severe challenges for Japanese archaeology. Earthquakes can damage or destroy heritage and archaeological sites. In recent times, they have also become a galvanizing influence, spurring on archaeological excavations in the affected regions.

The Great East Japan Earthquake of

ABOVE LEFT
A reconstruction of a Toro pit dwelling. It is still unclear how big the original settlement was.

ABOVE RIGHT
One of the turrets of Kumamoto Castle that was badly damaged in the 2016 earthquake.

OPPOSITE
A bronze, circular mirror from the Kofun period.

2011 devastated a vast area of the country, particularly Iwate, Miyagi and Fukushima Prefectures. The resulting tsunami reached more than 98½ ft (30 m) in height and swept several miles inland, destroying everything in its path. Almost 20,000 people were killed, and damage to the Fukushima No. 1 Nuclear Power Station led to serious radioactive contamination. In such tragic circumstances, damage to sites of cultural or historical interest may seem of minor concern. Yet damage there was, to more than 700 historic structures, including castles, fortresses, temples, shrines and other monuments. In Iwanuma City, the tsunami swept away ancient religious structures, and the Rikuzen-Takata municipal museum in Iwate was completely destroyed.

Another problem arose: Miyagi Prefecture has around 6,000 archaeological sites, and Iwate Prefecture has some 13,000, many of which have yet to be excavated. The majority of these sites are located in the hills above the devastated coastal plains – exactly where new homes were needed for those made homeless by the earthquake. So the authorities hastily recruited an archaeological labour force to excavate

as many of these sites as possible before construction work began on the new towns. It was a race against time, but the teams worked quickly and efficiently.

In Iwate, a total of 557,743 sq ft (170,000 sq m) was excavated prior to reconstruction at 30 sites. Many finds came to light as a result, altering understanding of local history. The archaeology teams held regular open days to share their discoveries with the public.

A similar emergency archaeology operation was carried out following the Great Hanshin Earthquake of 1995. Before the operation began, archaeologists were worried that they might be attacked by angry locals protesting at their presence in a disaster zone. To their surprise, the locals were fully supportive of the operation, and some 500 excavations were undertaken. The archaeologists who came out

following the 2011 earthquake were similarly well received.

The archaeologists at Fukushima faced a more challenging situation, because many sites had suffered radioactive contamination. By donning hazmat suits, they were able to go out and rescue archaeological objects and store these for future display.

Despite the challenges, archaeology has transformed our understanding of the Japanese past. Many impressive remains have been unearthed in Nara, the capital of Japan between 710 and 784, including Buddhist temples, Shinto shrines and the Heijō Imperial Palace. In 1998, the palace and the surrounding area were made a UNESCO World Heritage site. A reconstruction of the palace now exists on the site and in 2010 a series of festivals and cultural events commemorated the 1,300th anniversary of the movement of the capital to Heijō-kyō (now called Nara).

LEARNING FROM THE PAST

The 2011 earthquake inspired archaeologists, particularly in the Tohoku region, to go looking for traces of past earthquakes and tsunamis. They hoped that by uncovering evidence of these historic disasters, they might be able to help predict future ones. At Kutsukata, Sendai City, archaeologists found paddy fields dating from the middle Yayoi period, some 2,000 years ago. The fields were covered by a layer of white sand. By analysing the sand, they were able to determine that there had been a tsunami similar in scale to the 2011 one. In April 2014, the Nara National Research Institute for Cultural Properties began creating a database of historic natural disasters, recording the findings from Kutsukata and other places. A network of experts was set up to develop research methods and technologies for this new branch of geoarchaeology.

THE POMPEII OF JAPAN

Kanai Higashiura in Gunma Prefecture has been dubbed the Pompeii of Japan. Like the Roman city of Pompeii, the site was buried and preserved under ash from an erupting volcano. In Japan's case, the volcano was Harunayama Futatsudake, and the eruption took place in the early 6th century CE, during the Kofun period. In the course of excavating the site in 2012, archaeologists discovered the well-preserved remains of a Japanese warrior wearing body armour. This kind of armour is known as *kozaneko*, and suggests a soldier of high rank. Many examples of *kozaneko* have been discovered over the years, but none until this one were worn by their owner. From his position, the soldier must have been brave, for he appeared to be on his knees facing the volcano when he was engulfed by the flood of molten rock and ash. Archaeologists have speculated that he may have been praying, trying to calm the volcano's wrath.

THE COMPLEXITIES OF THE EAST

Much of southeast Asia's rich archaeological legacy is under-explored compared with sites in Europe and the Americas, because governments in the region have devoted fewer resources to archaeological research. As a result, there may be many exciting discoveries still to be made, with the potential to shed new light on the region's history.

BELOW LEFT
King An Duong Vuong temple in Co Loa, near Hanoi, an ancient fortress and first capital of independent Vietnam.

BELOW
Bronze drums from Co Loa, now at Hanoi Museum.

people constantly at war with their powerful northern neighbour. Instead, it suggests that the Vietnamese traded and coexisted with the Chinese for much of their history.

DATING CONTROVERSY

Ban Chiang, in Nong Han District, Thailand, is perhaps the most famous Bronze Age site in all of Southeast Asia. It is also one of the most controversial. In August 1966, an anthropology student named Steve Young was living in Ban Chiang interviewing people for his senior honours thesis. While walking along a path, Young tripped over a tree root. On the ground, he saw the exposed top of a ceramic jar. After digging it out, Young noticed it had been fired using primitive

SUPPORTING HISTORY?

Traditional histories of Vietnam tell of semi-legendary great kings nobly fighting for independence from their great northern neighbour, China. By contrast, early Chinese histories of the Vietnamese depict them as a savage people in need of civilizing. In the 1960s and 1970s, the Vietnamese government funded archaeological excavations seeking evidence to support the "great kings" theory of Vietnam's history Excavations were carried out at Co Loa, some 10 miles (16 km) north of Hanoi, on the Red River Delta. The delta is regarded by the Vietnamese as the birthplace of their civilization. The archaeologists were looking for evidence of a great civilization that might have flourished during the "middle phase" of Vietnamese history – after Neolithic

times, but before the period of Chinese domination from 111 BCE.

What the archaeologists found did not support either the "great kings" or the "savages" version of Vietnamese history. They did not discover the ruins of splendid cities, but they did find walls built over a period of almost 60 years. A multigenerational project on this scale was most likely created by a complex society concerned with strengthening security and controlling its resources. The team also found tiles very similar to Chinese tiles long pre-dating the actual influx of their northern neighbours. This contradicted the traditional image of a fiercely independent

techniques, but the design on the surface was unique and extraordinary.

The following year, a systematic excavation of the site unearthed human skeletons, together with bronze grave goods and grains of rice. At first, archaeologists concluded it was a cemetery, but evidence of dwellings was later found, suggesting that the dead were buried next to or beneath their homes.

Archaeologists used thermoluminescence dating on the ceramic pots. This technique involves heating the ceramic and then measuring the amount of light it emits. This indicates the amount of electric charge that has built up within it and therefore its age. The result was quite a shock: the pots were dated to 4420–3400 BCE,

making this the earliest Bronze Age culture in the world!

When a second excavation was carried out in 1974–5, sufficient organic material (rice and bone fragments) was collected from the site to carry out radiocarbon dating. The results suggested the site was more recent, with the oldest graves dating to about 2100 BCE, and the most recent to about 200 CE, while the earliest bronze objects were dated to 2000 BCE.

The new dates were not accepted by everyone, and it led to a heated debate about the site and its age. Over the years, evidence from subsequent excavations at this and other similar sites has given further support to the theory that Ban Chiang is a more recent settlement.

TEMPLES IN THE VALLEY

The rich Buddhist and Hindu heritage of Southeast Asia is preserved in the many elaborate temples that dot the landscape. In Cambodia, the Angkor Wat complex is the largest religious monument in the world and attracts thousands of tourists each year (see page 216). While pavements, roads and storerooms may have been reclaimed by the jungle, the temples continue to stand proud.

The medieval history of Myanmar, from around 600 to 1600 CE is the history of numerous peoples competing for the same territory along the fertile Irrawaddy River valley. They included the Mon, the Pyu, the Nan Chao, the Burmese, the Arakanese and the Shan. The most impressive legacies, however, were left by the Pyu, who dominated from 600 to 849, and the Burmese, who gained power from 849 to the late 1200s, centred on the city of Bagan, and who still dominate the country today. All

ABOVE
The remains of a wall which formed part of the ancient Pyu settlement of Sri Ksetra in Myanmar.

RIGHT
An example of a Pyu inscription from Hanlin, Myanmar.

KAMBAWZATHADI ROYAL PALACE

The Kambawzathadi Royal Palace in Bago was built in 1556 by King Bayinnaung, founder of the second Burmese kingdom. The enormous palace contained 76 halls and apartments. The palace burned down in 1599, but excavation of the site was carried out in the 1990s, during which some 1800 limestone sculptures of Buddha were unearthed. Based on knowledge gained from the excavations and original drawings of the building, part of the palace was reconstructed, including the Great Audience Hall and Bee Throne Hall.

of these cultures have been the focus of extensive archaeological excavations in Myanmar.

Tharay-khit-taya, situated 5 miles (8 km) from the modern town of Pyay in the north of the Irrawaddy, was the largest city of the Pyu. Intermittent archaeological work began here in 1907. Since 1964, archaeologists have worked intensively on the site, excavating and preserving monuments. Their efforts have revealed a circular city measuring 2¾ miles (4.4 km) in diameter, surrounded by a brick wall with 64 gates. The city contains stupas, pagodas, temples, residential buildings, a palace and 53 burial mounds. Archaeologists have found gold, bronze and stone statues, inscriptions in three languages, and urns inscribed with the names of kings and their dates.

Bagan was the capital of the first Burmese kingdom (known as Pagan). Most of its monuments were built between the 11th and 13th centuries when the kingdom was at its height. It rivals Angkor Wat in terms of its archaeological significance. More than 10,000 Buddhist temples, pagodas and monasteries were built in Bagan and its surrounding plains and the ruins of over 2,200 structures survive to this day. Ancient objects are preserved and displayed in the Bagan Archaeological Museum, established in 1902.

MEGALITHIC MONUMENTS

Indonesia is rich in archaeological sites from every era of history. One of its most famous is the megalithic site of Gunung Padang in West Java, some 31 miles (50 km) southwest of the city of Cianjur. Completed in about 5000 BCE, Gunang Padang is the largest megalithic site in all of Southeast Asia.

The complex consists of a terraced hill covering some 62 acres (25 hectares). Massive volcanic stones have been placed at the summit, which is surrounded by stone retaining walls that can be reached via 400 rock steps rising 311½ ft (95 m). Locals regard Gunang Padang as s acred. According to folklore, it was built by King Siliwangi in a single night. It was not properly studied until 1979.

A 2012 survey revealed that its earliest parts date back 12,500 years. Artefacts found near the surface date to about 2800 BCE. Traces of 9,000-year-old glue have also been discovered, used to stick rocks together. Ground penetrating radar revealed a large structure 49 ft (15 m) beneath the surface of the hill. According

ABOVE
Kambawzathadi Golden Palace in Bago, Myanmar, built by King Bayinnaung in the 16th century.

FOLLOWING PAGES
A truly amazing array of temples adorns the landscape at Bagan, the first capital of Myanmar.

ABOVE
Visitors explore the fourth terrace of the Gunung Padang Megalithic site, in the province of West Java in Indonesia.

to geologist Dr Danny Hilman, the structure may contain chambers, terraces and rooms with steps. Hilman speculates that it could be a temple, built between 9,000 and 20,000 years ago. He has even suggested that the entire hill is an ancient pyramid. If true, this could indicate the existence of a hitherto unknown prehistoric civilization on Java with advanced engineering skills.

Others are more sceptical that such a civilization could exist, especially as there is no other evidence of its structures in the area. A set of primitive 9,000-year-old tools found in a nearby cave suggest that a simpler culture existed at this site.

TOMBS AND TEMPLES

In the Bujang Valley in Malaysia, a sprawling complex of ancient ruins dates back more than 2,500 years. It covers an area of around 86½ sq miles (224 sq km), extending from Mount Jerai in the north to the Sungai River in the south. Archaeologists have unearthed more than 50 tomb-temples, called *candi* (pronounced "chandi"). Excavations have also revealed jetty remains, iron-smelting sites and a clay-brick monument. The Bujang Valley Archaeological Museum, located on the site, houses many of the artefacts discovered there, including inscribed stone tablets and caskets, metal tools, ceramics, pottery and Hindu icons.

During the 1950s and 1960s, research in the Bujang Valley was led by Western archaeologists including Horace Quaritch Wales, Dorothy Wales and Alistair Lamb. Since the 1970s, local archaeologists have continued the work there. With the support of the Malaysian government, they have carried out excavations and reconstructions. Since 2008, a team of Malaysian archaeologists have been excavating a port settlement in the Bujang Valley. In 2010, they unearthed a 1,900-year-old clay-brick monument built with geometric precision, possibly used for sun worship.

There have been setbacks: in December 2013, archaeologists at the site were outraged when a land developer demolished a 1,200-year-old Hindu temple (Candi No. 11). When challenged, the state government claimed the land was privately owned, so it was powerless to prevent it. In the wake of the controversy, Malaysia's Tourism and Heritage Ministry is considering declaring the Bujang Valley a heritage site, which will protect it from any future private development schemes.

THE RICHES OF THE CAVES

The Manunggul cave complex in Lipuun Point, Palawan, in the Philippines was explored by a team led by Dr Robert Fox between 1962 and 1965. The team found human remains covered in red paint and wearing bracelets of jade, shells and stone beads. They also discovered an extraordinary burial jar, the Manunggul Jar. The lid featured a sculpture of a "spirit boat" carrying two souls to the afterlife. In 1965, Fox explored the Leta-Leta Cave in northern Palawan, a burial site dating to 1000–1500 BCE containing many stone and pottery artefacts. These included the famous "yawning jarlet of Leta-Leta", the earliest known pot in the Philippines.

In 2007, a team led by Dr Armand

BELOW
Hindu-Buddhist archaeological ruins in Bujang Valley in the Malaysian state of Kedah that are more than 2,500 years old.

CITY OF TEMPLES

The modern state of Cambodia was dominated in the medieval period by the Khmer people. The greatest legacy of the Khmer is the Hindu temple complex of Angkor Wat, the largest religious monument in the world. Spread over a site of 403 acres (163 hectares), it is admired for its magnificent architecture and the beautiful carvings on its walls.

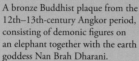

BELOW
A bronze Buddhist plaque from the 12th–13th-century Angkor period, consisting of demonic figures on an elephant together with the earth goddess Nan Brah Dharani.

Angkor Wat is one of the most important archaeological sites in Southeast Asia, and the focus of on-going study. In 1997, a team of archaeologists launched the Greater Angkor Project (GAP) to map the surrounding landscape, using ground surveys, aerial photographs and ground-penetrating radar. The project, completed in 2007, revealed that Angkor was far bigger than previously suspected. In fact, at its peak in the 12th century, it was the largest urban centre on Earth, with a population of around one million living in a network of suburbs.

The survey picked out 74 temple sites, more than 1,000 artificial ponds and a massive water system that linked the entire conurbation, supplying the Angkor residents with constant water, as well as irrigation for

ABOVE
The majestic sight of the Ta Prohm Temple at Angkor Wat where, over time, trees have become fused into the structure of the building.

LEFT
A bas-relief carving depicting Khmer culture, in Angkor Wat.

their crops. Angkor's success may have proved its undoing: the research showed evidence of overpopulation leading to deforestation and topsoil degradation that may have brought about Angkor's collapse.

Further studies of the site were carried out in 2012 and 2015 using cutting-edge airborne laser scanning (LiDAR) technology. By firing lasers at the ground from a helicopter, researchers were able to produce detailed imagery of sub-surface ruins. The laser scans identified earthen embankments built in geometric patterns, which may once have been gardens. They found evidence of towers that had been built and demolished during the construction of Angkor Wat, and a massive structure of unknown purpose to the south of the temple complex. The scans also revealed an area of low-density residential housing, with a road grid, ponds and mounds, possibly used by people working in the temple.

Mijares, discovered a foot bone in Callao Cave near Peñablanca, Cagayan. The bone turned out to be 67,000 years old, making it the earliest known human fossil found in the entire Asia-Pacific region.

In Butuan City in 2012, archaeologists recovered the remains of an enormous boat called a *balangay*. The boat, estimated to be around 82 ft (25 m) long, could be up to 800 years old, long predating the European ships that landed in the Philippines in the 16th century.

The earliest known document in the country is the Laguna Copper Plate, dated to around 900 CE. It was accidentally discovered in 1986 near the mouth of the Lumbang river. Written in Kavi, an old Javanese writing system, it turned out to be a receipt for the payment of a debt.

ABOVE
Cave explorers in Callao Cave at Cagayan in the Philippines.

OPPOSITE ABOVE
The Laguna Copper Plate, found in the Lumbang river in the Philippines.

OPPOSITE BELOW
The Manunggul Jar, a Neolithic burial jar dating from c.890–710 BCE.

THE LIMESTONE TOMBS OF KAMHANTIK

Perhaps the most extraordinary of recent archaeological finds in the Philippines took place in 2011 on a jungle-covered mountain in Kamhantik. Here, archaeologists from the country's National Museum unearthed the remains of a village that could be up to 1000 years old. At the site, they found 15 large limestone coffins dating to between the 10th and 14th centuries. The dating was based on an analysis of a human tooth found in one of the tombs. If it's correct, this would make them the earliest known limestone tombs in the Philippines. Evidence from other sites of this era indicates that early Filipinos used wooden coffins. The limestone tombs were rectangular, resembling Egyptian sarcophagi, though simpler in design and with no ornamentation. Metal tools must have been used to carve them, indicating that the indigenous population was more technologically advanced than previously realized. Inside the tombs, the archaeologists found thousands of sherds of earthenware jars, metal objects and the bone fragments of humans, monkeys, wild pigs and other animals.

Manunggul Jar

THE SPLENDOURS OF SOUTH ASIA

As the location of one of the world's earliest civilizations, the Indus Valley (see pages 116–25), the history of South Asia (encompassing the present-day countries of Afghanistan, Bangladesh, Bhutan, India, the Maldives, Nepal and Sri Lanka) is a long one. The earliest known accounts of visitors to the area stretch back to that of Xuanzang, who came from China in the 7th century. Following him came others, such as Marco Polo, Ibn Battuta and Vasco da Gama.

BELOW LEFT
The Italian mercenary Jean-Baptiste Ventura spent his spare time excavating *stupas* in the Khyber Pass.

BELOW
Alexander Cunningham (fourth from right), the first Director of the Archaeological Survey of India.

A WESTERN OBSESSION

Archaeological work in the area was first recorded in the 18th century. Sir William Jones founded the Asiatic Society in Calcutta in 1784 to promote the cause of Oriental research. Among the first Europeans to undertake excavations was Jean-Baptiste Ventura, an Italian mercenary hired to help modernize the Sikh army. He spent his spare time in Peshawar, excavating *stupas* in the Khyber Pass, in which he discovered Greek coins. In turn, he inspired

the work of Alexander Cunningham, who in 1861 became the first Surveyor General and Director of the Archaeological Survey of India, which is responsible to this day for all archaeological work in India.

Alexander Cunnngham became fascinated with Buddhist culture. As director of the Archaeological Survey of India, he led excavations at Sarnath and Bodh Gaya. He rediscovered Nalanda, a site that goes back to the time of the Buddha. There he excavated temples and palaces in two parallel rows, many of them with sculptural panels and elaborate walls of carved bead-and-reel decorations and wheel-and-dear insignia, along with plentiful evidence of early bronze casting.

Following in Cunningham's footsteps came the likes of Robert Bruce Foote, and Sir John Marshall, with the latter adding extensively to the history of South Asian civilization with his meticulous excavations at Mohenjo-Daro and Harappa.

INDIAN EMPIRES

| 323 BCE–185 BCE Mauryan Empire | 30–375 CE Kushan Empire | 320–550 CE Gupta Empire | 606–647 Empire of Harsha | 1206–1526 Delhi Sultanate | 1526–40, 1555–1857 Mughal Empire | 1645–1818 Maratha Empire |

ABOVE
The impressive temples at Nalanda were excavated by Alexander Cunningham, who had developed a fascination with Buddhism during his time in India.

LEFT
The *Rig Veda* is one of the oldest surviving texts from any Indo-European language.

THE *RIG VEDA*

The *Rig Veda* consists of 1,028 hymns dedicated to the multitude of deities of the Aryan peoples who appeared in India for the first time in about 1500 BCE. It can scarcely be regarded as an historical record: not only is there no attempt at any kind of history telling, but it is also widely assumed to have been written down several hundred years after the period it refers to. Its importance, however, is that it was written in Sanskrit, the language of the Aryans and the distant ancestor of Greek and Latin. *Veda*, for example, is simply the Sanskrit word for "knowledge".

MANY EMPIRES

After the disappearance of the Indus Valley civilizations came what has been called the Indian Dark Age, which began at some point around 1500 BCE. A written record of sorts exists of these turbulent centuries. This is the Hindu *Rig Veda*, the oldest religious text in the world, composed between 1700 and 1100 BCE. In every important respect, it marks the birth of Hinduism, and the India that emerged in the confused and hazy aftermath of the Indus Valley civilizations.

It was a period that saw the rise and fall of a series of north Indian empires and the settlement of much of the south of India, particularly around Chennai, Mysuru and Kerala. Here, however, hilly and often impenetrable jungle militated against the development of larger political entities. Critically, however, even in the north where central control was strongest, India was increasingly marked by a religious diversity that continues to this day.

The major theme that emerges from the first part of this period is the appearance of the Aryans and their gradual eastward settlement of the river valleys of the Yamuna and, especially,

the Ganges, both flowing into the Bay of Bengal. This eastward movement is amply attested by finds of pottery known as Painted Grey Ware. Two sites stand out: Mathura, claimed as the birthplace of the Hindu god Krishna; and Ahichatra, the latter inhabited continuously from 600 BCE to 1100 CE and first excavated from 1940 to 1944.

In addition to the Aryans' development of an extraordinarily complicated metaphysical belief system, what most obviously characterized the early centuries of Aryan settlement was their protracted struggle with the native Dasas. The latter's eventual defeat was possibly the origin of the Hindu caste system as the Dasas became the untouchables.

The settlement of the Ganges was evidently well under way before

ABOVE
This pottery fragment is an example of the Painted Grey Ware culture.

LEFT
The religious temple at Mathura, claimed as the birthplace of the god Krishna, is one of the most popular religious sites in India.

RIGHT
This icon of a goddess with
weapons bursting from her hair
comes from the Magadhan capital
of Pataliputra.

FAR RIGHT
An example of a stone pillar (see
overleaf) built during the rule of
Asoka at Vaishali.

1000 BCE. It was critically dependent on the growth of rice, which became the staple crop of the region. Nonetheless, by 500 BCE, a more-or-less well-defined series of 16 states or "mahajanapadas" had emerged across the Gangetic plains. Their numbers were then gradually reduced to four, of which Magadha, with a substantial capital on the banks of the Ganges, Pataliputra, would emerge at the end of the 4th century BCE as the core of the first great Indian empire, the Mauryan. Hardly less important, it was

here that both Buddhism and Jainism were developed.

The Mauryan empire was the creation of a prince, Chandragupta. *Circa* 325 BCE he staged a coup, seizing the throne of Magadha and then extending its rule well to the east and the south. Pataliputra remains the most obvious expression of this first phase of Mauryan rule. Though much lies underneath today's city of Patna, what has been excavated reveals a city of astonishing size and sumptuousness.

Mauryan India reached its peak under the rule of Chandragupta's grandson, Asoka, in the 3rd century BCE. As his empire grew, so Pataliputra grew, too. It was claimed to have held a population in excess of 150,000 and its wooden walls had "570 towers and 64 gates". No less important, its architecture, especially the monument called the "Pataliputra capital", betrays clear Persian and Greek influences, the result of Alexander the Great's conquests first of Persia, then of India, where he reached the Indus in

327 BCE. It presaged a cultural exchange between the Middle East and northern India that would endure for centuries.

At least as lasting an influence from Asoka was his championing of Buddhism. It was made possible by an exceptionally well-organized administrative system, one set out in a work known as the *Arthashastra*, written by Chandragupta's chief minister, Kautilya. It resulted in the building of an estimated 84,000 *stupa*, hemispherical monuments built either of stone or brick and generally containing relics, sometimes burials. The most celebrated is that at Sanchi, built and rebuilt between the 3rd century BCE and the 12th century CE. No less characteristic was the construction of a series of imposing stone pillars, similarly proclaiming Buddhist teachings, many topped by lions and/or a wheel, symbolizing the world. Asoka himself was hailed as a *chakravartin*, or "wheel turner".

The Mauryan empire was shortlived. It was followed by a confused series of invasions and settlements, of territorial seizures and sudden collapses. The most enduring of these settlements was the Kushana empire that in the 300 years up

THE SANCHI MONASTERY

The enduring significance of Asoka's embrace of Buddhism found expression in his creation of a series of monasteries. Of them, that at Sanchi in central India, rebuilt in the 1st century CE, remains the most commanding. It is in the form of a stupa, a symbolic structure, a hemispherical dome, raised over holy relics and acting as "an architectural diagram of the cosmos", with the dome a representation of the heavens. Circling it is an immense stone fence, pierced by four gates, each aligned to the four cardinal points of the compass. It was only in 1912, when the site was taken over by the Archaeological Survey of India, that the first serious attempts at its preservation were made.

to approximately 300 CE laid claim to most of northwest India. The rise of the Roman empire at least re-established the sub-continent's trading links to the wider world. By the 1st century CE, Pliny in Rome was bemoaning the excessive cost of imported luxury Indian goods. In turn, the Mediterranean shipped wines, copper, dates, slaves and pearls to India. Overland trade with China similarly burgeoned.

A further empire followed, that of the Guptas, who from about 300 CE took over and extended Pataliputra, from where they ruled an empire that almost rivalled the Mauryan in extent. Their energetic promotion of Hinduism has led many to call Gupta India the Classical Age of India. In fact, Gupta rule never extended to the southern tip of the sub-continent, where prosperity was markedly increased both in and around Madras and in Sri Lanka, and it was brought to a sudden and violent end in about 480 CE.

Nomadic warrior invaders from Central Asia, the White Huns, descended on India. India was reduced to "a patchwork of petty kingdoms squabbling among themselves". It would take until the 16th century for India to re-emerge on the world stage.

Holy Men and Sages

As early as 327 BCE, when Alexander the Great reached the borders of India on his epic campaigns, India's reputation in the Ancient World as a land celebrated for its holy men and sages was already established.

Buddhism spread astonishingly rapidly across much of east and southeast Asia. Mahayana Buddhism placed great importance on images of the Buddha himself. The creation of such images was considered a worthy deed in itself. Thus, from the 1st century CE, it led to a proliferation of carved images of the Buddha and those semi-divine beings, the Bodhisattvas, across central India.

Of the multitude of surviving examples, the oldest was discovered in 2013 at Lumbini in Nepal, traditionally claimed as the birthplace of Siddhartha Gautama, the Buddha himself. The excavations were undertaken by a team led by British archaeologist Robin Coningham. If its provisional date of 550 BCE is correct, it would mean that 563 BCE, the date traditionally said to mark the birth of Siddhartha Gautama, might be too late by perhaps a century, as ritual practices of Buddhism were already well underway.

The vast majority of such images were produced only from the 1st century BCE. There were two main centres: Gandhara, an area that straddles northwest India as well as parts of Pakistan and Afghanistan; and the northern Indian city of Mathura. The Gandhara statues show clear influences of Greek statuary. The finest example, dating from the 2nd or 3rd centuries BCE, is held in the British Museum in London. It comes from a Buddhist monastery at Jamal

Garhi, close to the town of Mardan in Pakistan. The monastery was discovered in 1848 by Alexander Cunningham. It was 10 years later that the statue itself, along with many others, was discovered during an archaeological expedition led by another British army officer, Lieutenant Cromten.

OPPOSITE
Carving images of the Buddha was seen as a worthy endeavour.

ABOVE
The world's tallest statue of the Buddha was carved into a cliff face in Bamiyan in central Afghanistan but destroyed by the Taliban in 2001.

Heritage at risk

At Bamiyan in central Afghanistan, two Buddhas were carved in the 6th century CE into a cliff face, one 115 ft (35 m) high, the other 174 ft (53 m) high. In 2001, both were destroyed by the Taliban. The resulting international outrage led to a sustained archaeological effort that in 2004 revealed the existence of 50 hitherto unknown caves, in 12 of which wall paintings of Buddhas were discovered. Painted with an oil-based mixture, they have been confirmed as the oldest-known oil paintings in the world.

A no less remarkable example of the vivid tradition of Buddhist visual art is provided by the Ajanta caves in Maharashtra in western Indian. In Western terms, they were discovered in 1819 by yet another British army officer, John Smith. The work of creating the caves was concentrated into a relatively brief period between 460 and 480 BCE.

These and other examples of early craftsmanship were the precursors of the artistic work created in the centuries that followed, including that of the Mughal Empire, renowned for its artwork.

RIGHT
An intricate statue of the Buddha lies in the centre of the Ajanta caves in western India.